quick-fix
vegetarian

Other Books by Robin Robertson

Peanut Butter Planet

Apocalypse Chow! (with Jon Robertson)

Carb-Conscious Vegetarian

Fresh from the Vegetarian Slow Cooker

Vegan Planet

The Vegetarian Meat and Potatoes Cookbook

Pasta for All Seasons

Rice and Spice

The Sacred Kitchen (with Jon Robertson)

The Vegetarian Chili Cookbook

Some Like It Hot

The Soy Gourmet

366 Simply Delicious Dairy-Free Recipes

366 Healthful Ways to Cook Tofu and Other Meat Alternatives

healthy
home-cooked
meals in

30 minutes
or less

quick-fix
vegetarian

robin robertson

Andrews McMeel
Publishing, LLC
Kansas City

09 10 11 RR2 10 9 8 7 6 5

ISBN-13: 978-0-7407-6374-8
ISBN-10: 0-7407-6374-1

Library of Congress Cataloging-in-Publication Data
Robertson, Robin (Robin G.)
Quick-fix vegetarian / Robin Robertson.
p. cm.
ISBN-13: 978-0-7407-6374-8
ISBN-10: 0-7407-6374-1
1. Vegetarian cookery.   2. Quick and easy cookery.   I. Title.
TX837.R624974 2007
641.5'636--dc22

                                    2006051016

All photos © istockphoto.com

www.andrewsmcmeel.com

ATTENTION: SCHOOLS AND BUSINESSES
Andrews McMeel books are available at quantity discounts with bulk purchase for educational, business, or sales promotional use. For information, please write to: Special Sales Department, Andrews McMeel Publishing, LLC, 1130 Walnut Street, Kansas City, Missouri 64106.

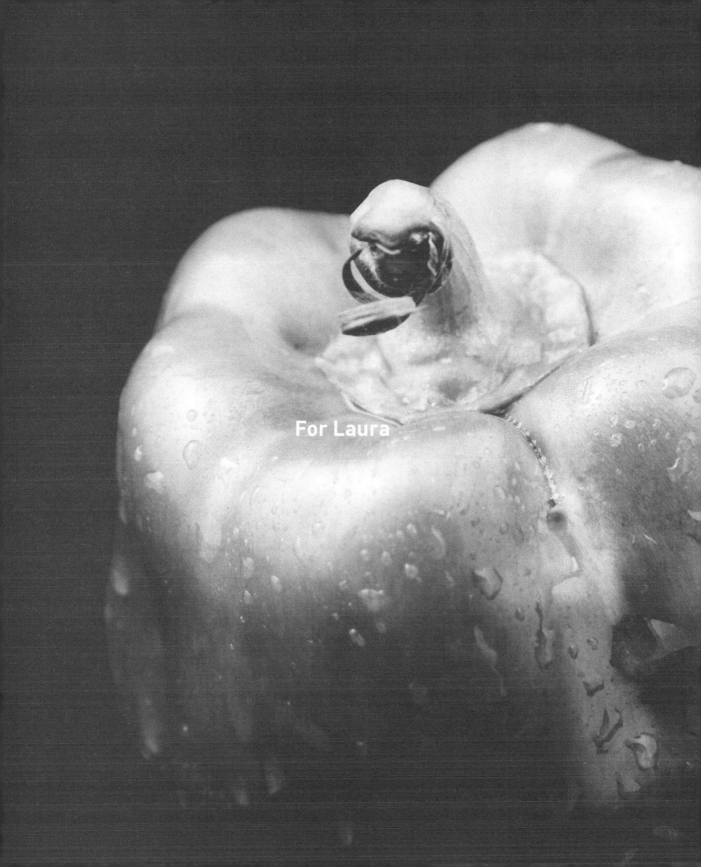

For Laura

contents

acknowledgments

Many people helped make this book a reality. Much gratitude goes to my wonderful recipe testers: Janet Aaronson, Sandy Boss, Julie Bouchet-Horwitz, Kim Hammond, Clinton Hedges, Lauren Horwitz, Sarah King, Sangeeta Kumar, Linda Levy, Gina Myers, and Anna West, with a special thanks to supertester Laura Frisk, who single-handedly tested more than one-third of these recipes and to whom this book is dedicated. Many thanks to my husband, Jon Robertson, for his ongoing encouragement and assistance and to my friend Jannette Patterson for her help and support. Thanks also to my agent, Stacey Glick, of Dystel & Goderich Literary Management, and to my editor, Jean Lucas, of Andrews McMeel Publishing, for their enthusiasm for this project.

introduction

People are always looking for ways to spend less time in the kitchen, and the unlimited offerings of frozen entrées in our supermarkets and the ubiquity of fast-food restaurants have made it possible. As a result, however, many of us no longer cook the way we used to. At the same time, it is clear that eating healthier food is vitally important for everyone, especially those who lead busy lives.

To eat better, many people are turning to a vegetarian diet, and the good news is that cooking great vegetarian food has never been easier. Once considered a labor-intensive chore, preparing vegetarian meals can now be pared down to fit even the busiest schedule.

With *Quick-Fix Vegetarian*, you will no longer be limited to microwave entrées and fast-food chains for an easy solution to putting dinner on the table. Whether you're a novice or a seasoned vegetarian, the recipes, tips, and ideas in this book will turn you into a "quick-fix vegetarian" cook in no time. You will discover the simple techniques, shortcuts, and strategies so "fast food" no longer has to mean "junk" food.

During my years as a restaurant chef, I learned how to cook smarter, not harder—when it was my job to prepare meals for customers within ten to fifteen minutes, I learned a lot of

time-saving tricks. Now that I'm working at home, it's important to me to prepare healthful meals each day, but I rarely have the time to spend the day in the kitchen fussing over time-consuming recipes. That doesn't mean that I toss frozen entrées in the microwave or keep my local Chinese takeout on speed-dial. I've discovered something better: good-for-you "fast food" that you prepare yourself, economically, and in record time. Flavorful soups, tempting salads, rich sauces, fabulous entrées, and elegant desserts—all designed to get you in and out of the kitchen in thirty minutes or less.

The 150 delicious and satisfying recipes in *Quick-Fix Vegetarian* call for fresh produce, grains, pastas, and beans, along with healthy convenience foods and time-saving shortcuts to help you prepare tasty and nutritious meals when there's little time to cook. At the same time, *Quick-Fix Vegetarian* can help you master the art of healthy and flavorful meals with new shopping and cooking strategies as well as creative tips for stress-free entertaining. The recipes contain no animal ingredients, so they are ideal to serve to vegans and those who are lactose-intolerant.

Quick-Fix Vegetarian can be an invaluable resource to both novices and longtime vegetarians, offering easy ways to integrate smart eating into your life every day and in less time than it takes to have a pizza delivered. With uncomplicated main-dish recipes such as Rapini with Orzo and Sun-Dried Tomatoes, Capellini with White Bean and Green Olive Tapenade, and Five-Minute Slow-Cooker Chili, *Quick-Fix Vegetarian* can simplify your life and help you put great meals on the table with a minimum of time and effort.

quick-fix
vegetarian

chapter 1

a quick-fix vegetarian kitchen

To some people, a meal isn't quick unless they pick it up at a drive-through window or nuke it in the microwave. As much as they'd love to put a home-cooked meal on the table every night, they complain that there's just no time to cook. With *Quick-Fix Vegetarian*, the "no time to cook" excuse can be a thing of the past.

The recipes in this book are designed to make great-tasting vegetarian food as easy and excuse-proof as possible. Let's face it, when getting dinner on the table is faster than ordering takeout, the choice is easy. When you prepare "quick-fix" recipes, you're not just saving time, you also have the satisfaction of enjoying delicious home-cooked meals that are healthier and more economical than takeout.

That's why I developed these quick-cooking recipes for appetizers, soups, salads, main dishes, and desserts that take less than thirty minutes to prepare. Before delving into the recipes themselves, I'd like to share some kitchen tips and time-saving strategies as well as information about the ingredients and the recipes.

A "quick-fix" kitchen is about more than easy-to-prepare recipes with short cooking times. It's also about keeping a pantry well stocked with meal-enhancing ingredients that

can help you save preparation time, keeping a well-organized kitchen, and assembling your ingredients before beginning a recipe. It's also about incorporating strategies such as having sharp knives and other time-saving equipment, as well as menu planning and the judicious use of convenience foods, many of which are called for in the recipes in this book. For those who prefer to prepare these convenience foods at home, I provide recipes for making many of them from scratch, along with descriptions of their store-bought counterparts.

about the recipes

First, I'd like to clarify what I mean by "less than thirty minutes" to make these recipes. That time includes both the preparation and the cooking, although it doesn't include the time it takes to gather your equipment and ingredients or to wash your produce.

As a time-saving cooking strategy, consider washing and drying your produce when you bring it home from the store. That way, your ingredients are ready when you need them. (Notable exceptions to this suggestion are fragile items such as mushrooms and berries that should only be washed just prior to use.)

At the end of certain recipes, I've listed "Quicker Fix" notes. These refer to optional shortcuts that may be taken, such as using a prepared product in place of a homemade one. I've incorporated as many of these shortcuts into the recipes as possible without compromising the recipe quality.

Exceptions to the "less than thirty minutes from start to finish" rule are recipes that benefit from extra chilling time, such as gazpacho, as well as the slow-cooker and oven-baked recipes that are included in this book. For those recipes, the prep time is under thirty minutes, but the cooking takes longer.

I especially like the inclusion of slow-cooker and oven-baked recipes in the "quick-fix" repertoire because they take only a few minutes of preparation time. Once you put them on to cook, your work is done until it's time to eat. In some ways, they can actually be more convenient than recipes made at the last minute, because you get to decide when to do the prep—at your own convenience, not right before dinner when everyone is starving.

selected shortcuts

My work as a restaurant chef taught me a number of time-saving tricks, many of which can be adapted for the home kitchen. One important key to saving time in the kitchen is being organized. A great way to do this is to assemble your *mise en place*, which means gathering ingredients and equipment needed before beginning a recipe, including measuring out the ingredients. This kitchen time-saver is standard procedure in restaurant kitchens and cooking schools.

Another way to save time is to read and reread the recipe you will be using. When you are familiar with your recipe, and you have your ingredients and equipment at hand, you will be amazed at how much more easily you can prepare a meal. Good prep can also help avoid kitchen mishaps, such as missing ingredients, wrong pans, or dinner being burned up while you search for a spice or a spatula. If you do your *mise en place* prior to making each recipe, it will save you time and may also bump up the quality of your cooking.

I also encourage you to practice being a more intuitive or instinctive cook. By this, I mean don't be afraid to substitute or change ingredients when it seems appropriate. For example, if you don't like a certain ingredient in a recipe, just make a reasonable substitution for something you do like, such as replacing tarragon with basil or pinto beans with kidney beans. In most cases, the recipe will turn out just as well; maybe better, since it will now have your own personal touch.

The same is true if you find that you're out of an ingredient when you're ready to prepare dinner. While it's best to plan ahead and make sure in advance that you have everything you need in the house, sometimes it just happens that we run out of an ingredient at the last minute. In those cases, rather than dropping everything to rush out to the store, try to determine if you have something in the house that can be substituted. To avoid running out of the ingredients you use most frequently, keep an ongoing grocery list in the kitchen so you can write down items the minute you run out.

In addition to cooking the "quick-fix" recipes in this book, there are a number of other ways you can get dinner on the table in less time. From convenience-food meals to cooking marathons, here are some great quick-meal tips that can help you every time you plan your meals:

dinners of convenience

One of the best ways to get in and out of the kitchen quickly is by having a well-stocked pantry. In fact, there are a number of amazingly flavorful meals that can be made mostly with pantry ingredients that I've come to think of as convenience foods. Of course, my first choice will always be cooking with garden fresh or at least store-bought-fresh, preferably organic, ingredients, but for those times when I run out of fresh ingredients and need to put a meal together in a hurry, these pantry ingredients come in handy. Keep a supply of your favorite pantry items on hand, and there will always be the makings of a fine dinner at your fingertips.

One of my favorite pantry meals consists of sautéing garlic in olive oil and adding a can of artichoke hearts, a can of diced tomatoes, and some sliced black olives. You can also add some capers or chopped roasted red bell peppers, or maybe a can

of white beans and a few handfuls of baby spinach, if you have some. Simply toss this mixture with cooked pasta, and dinner is served. You can also use it as a topping for your favorite grain, or on veggie cutlets, bruschetta, tofu, or veggie burgers.

best-made plans: stocking the "quick-fix" vegetarian pantry

The better your kitchen is stocked, the more choices you will have at dinnertime. Here is a list of some ingredients and convenience foods that you can use to make a variety of "quick-fix" vegetarian meals described in this book. I don't list all the basic ingredients that every well-stocked kitchen has on hand, but rather the ingredients needed for the shortcuts provided in this book.

- **Canned beans:** Infinitely versatile and convenient, canned beans such as chickpeas, kidney beans, cannellini beans, black beans, and pintos add protein and nutrients to salads, pasta dishes, and grain and veggie dishes. In addition, they can be pureed to make sauces and dips or mashed to make burgers and loaves.

- **Bottled pasta sauce:** indispensable for making a quick and easy pasta meal. Doctor up the dish with a package of frozen veggie-burger crumbles or canned beans and a splash of red wine.

- **Cooked polenta:** available refrigerated in a log shape or boxed in a rectangular shape. Great topped with chili or a jar of marinara sauce combined with canned chickpeas or frozen veggie-burger crumbles.

- **Soft tortillas:** In addition to the usual burritos, fajitas, and quesadillas, use soft tortillas to make a variety of wrap sandwiches, layered casseroles, and even superthin-crust pizzas.

- **Quick-cooking grains and pastas:** couscous, bulgur, quick-cooking brown rice, pasta, rice sticks, soba (buckwheat) noodles

- **Frozen veggie-burger crumbles:** Widely available in natural food stores and supermarkets, the taste, texture, and convenience of this product makes this a great item to keep on hand for quick tacos, chili, sloppy joes, pasta sauce, lasagna, shepherd's pie, and more.

- **Tofu and tempeh:** nutritious soy foods widely available in supermarkets and natural food stores. These can be used in a variety of ways and are especially good as high-protein meat alternatives.

- **Seitan (wheat meat):** protein-rich meat alternative made from wheat. It is available refrigerated and frozen in natural food stores.

- **Veggie burgers:** In addition to cooking them as is, veggie burgers can be chopped and used to make chili, pasta sauce, or tacos or used in a stuffing for peppers or other vegetables. They can also be cut into strips for fajitas, slathered with barbecue sauce, and much more.

- **Pizza shells:** Buy ready-to-use pizza shells to make healthy custom pizzas topped with roasted or grilled veggies, pesto, veggie pepperoni, or your favorite topping combination.

meal enhancers

In addition to the convenience foods listed above, my kitchen arsenal includes a variety of exciting sauces and other ingredients that I use to dress up simple meals. Depending on your personal taste, consider keeping several of these ingredients on hand to lend variety to simple grain, pasta, and vegetable dishes as well as tofu, tempeh, seitan, and veggie burgers:

- Vegetable broth (cubes, powder, canned, aseptic carton)
- Canned tomato products (diced, whole, puree, paste)
- Nondairy milk: soy, rice, oat, almond (aseptic carton)
- Dried fruits: raisins, cranberries, apricots, etc.
- Light unsweetened coconut milk
- Tomato salsa
- Barbecue sauce
- Chili paste
- Hoisin sauce
- Tamari
- Teriyaki sauce
- Curry paste or powder
- Chutney
- Jerk sauce
- Peanut butter
- Tahini (sesame paste)
- Basil pesto
- Black and green olives
- Artichoke hearts (canned and frozen)
- Sun-dried tomatoes (dried and packed in oil)
- Roasted red bell peppers (bottled)

- Miso paste (light and dark)
- Vegetarian mushroom gravy
- Minced ginger (bottled)
- Black or green olive tapenade
- Soy mayonnaise
- Dried chiles
- Capers
- Almond butter
- Nuts and seeds

lists: grocery shopping and menu planning

A key element to stress-free meal planning involves making lists: an ongoing grocery list and a list of menu plans for the week. Here are some ideas on how to incorporate list-making into your routine:

- Keep a list of your family's favorite dishes and rotate them regularly.
- Plan meals in advance, serving make-ahead one-dish meals or "quick-fix" veggie burgers or stir-fries on especially busy nights.
- Plan your menus: This doesn't have to be a formal complete menu plan from soup to nuts, but it will help in grocery shopping and save you time for the rest of the week if you have a good idea of what you want to make for dinner. Just a simple jotting down of "Monday: pasta; Tuesday: vegetarian chili; Wednesday: tofu stir-fry; Thursday: veggie burgers," etc., will cue you as you make your grocery list to items you may need to buy to carry out your menu plan. Consider using a separate calendar just for menu planning.
- Writing out a menu list can help you write your grocery list and will cut down on unnecessary trips to the supermarket.

- Make a master grocery list once and photocopy it for future use.
- Keep your grocery list handy to jot items on the list as they become low.
- Keep your pantry shelves organized, so you know where things are at a glance.
- Stock up on healthy "convenience" foods, including canned beans, couscous, quick-cooking pastas, frozen veggie burger crumbles, and a variety of condiments.
- Keep convenience items on hand that add flavor to a recipe.
- Reduce the time you spend at the supermarket by becoming familiar with the store layout (many supermarkets have maps of their stores) and writing your grocery list in the same order as the store aisles. This will cut down on backtracking, such as when you discover on aisle 12 that you need the mustard back on aisle 2.
- You can make the most of the time spent at the supermarket by taking advantage of sales and having some flexibility regarding ingredient choices. For example, when the store has a sale on asparagus, you want to buy extra to enjoy before the price goes back up.

marathon cooking

Another strategy that can be used when time is at a premium is what I call "marathon cooking," in which you prepare several meals at once. It should be done at a time when you have a few hours to spend in the kitchen—I usually have my marathon session on a Sunday, when I put on some music and cook enough food to get me through the week. I like to prepare things that reheat well or that can be portioned and frozen. Some of my favorites include making a pot of vegetarian chili, a hearty vegetable soup, and a casserole or a grain pilaf. It's also a great time to cook a big batch of brown rice or dried beans.

Here are some guidelines for marathon cooking:

- Cook double batches of long-cooking recipes, such as vegetable stew, soup, and chili, that become more flavorful when reheated, so you can serve them again later in the week or freeze them for another time.
- Cook large amounts of grains and beans, then portion and freeze them for later use. That way, when you need them, they're already cooked.
- Combine prep work if making more than one recipe—for example, if you're making both chili and a soup, chop enough onion for both at the same time.
- Keep on hand a supply of perishable staples such as onions, carrots, and celery for a soup or stew, fresh lettuces and other salad ingredients, and a variety of vegetables and fruits.
- Wash lettuces and other vegetables when you bring them home from the store. This will save you time when you want to make a quick salad or cook a meal. Make sure to dry or spin them, too—otherwise they will spoil faster.

planning for leftovers

Instead of groaning at the thought of leftovers, I actually plan for them. I love leftovers. Certain dishes, like soups and stews, actually taste better to me the second time around. Still, many people don't like to eat the same thing two days in a row. In such cases, it only takes a little ingenuity to use up leftovers in creative ways.

One idea is to make dinner with a second meal in mind. This can give new life to your leftovers by transforming them into an entirely new dish. For example, you can use leftover vegetarian chili to make a layered Mexican-style casserole with soft tortillas, salsa, and other ingredients. Leftover vegetable stew can be transformed into a potpie with the simple addition of a ready-to-use piecrust topping. Leftover vegetable soup can be pureed into a flavorful primavera sauce for pasta. Leftover vegetables can be used in a quiche or added to composed salads or pasta and grain dishes. In the same way, leftover pasta, potatoes, or rice can be added to salads or soups for a hearty main-dish meal.

Whenever you cook, get into the habit of thinking about preparing food that can be incorporated into a second meal. Simply by making an entire box of pasta, when you may only need half for your initial recipe, you can save time by having the remaining cooked pasta available for another night to use in a different way.

about the ingredients

It was important to me to make this book as user-friendly as possible. For that reason, I've done my best to use easy-to-find ingredients in the recipes. I don't want someone not to try a recipe simply because she can't find a certain ingredient. A particular shortcut I take in many of the recipes is the use of organic canned beans and quick-cooking grains, as well as other ingredients such as vegetable broth and roasted red bell peppers. There are some people who admirably cook their beans and grains from scratch and make homemade stock. There is no question that this is the best choice both nutritionally and economically. However, with today's hectic pace, I'm just happy when people eat beans and grains at all. If preparing a meal with canned beans and quick-cooking rice prevents them from heading for the golden arches, then I'm all for it.

Ultimately, whether you want to cook your beans from scratch or open a can is up to you. In most cases, the recipes will call for the most convenient choice, but if you prefer to make certain ingredients from scratch, you can do so ahead of time and then dig into the recipe after you have cooked your beans, made your own vegetable stock, or roasted your own bell peppers, and so on. Recipes for several "make your own" basics can be found at the end of this chapter.

I like to use a few time-saving ingredients that are also quite economical. One of them is bottled minced ginger found in the produce section of many supermarkets. This product is of high quality and eliminates the need to buy a large piece of ginger that needs to be peeled and grated before using. It also cuts down on waste from peeling away too much or by allowing leftover ginger to shrivel in the refrigerator. Another handy ingredient to keep on hand is frozen bell pepper strips. I keep a bag of them in the freezer for times when I need only a small amount of bell pepper for a recipe, or when I've run out of fresh ones, or when fresh bell peppers are too expensive.

Likewise, peeled garlic cloves, available in jars in the produce section of the supermarket, are convenient time-savers and they taste great. While minced garlic is also available in jars, I prefer the flavor quality of the whole peeled garlic cloves. A jar of peeled garlic cloves can also be a handy backup when the remains of your fresh garlic bulb have sprouted or dried up.

A few other ingredient points: When salt is listed, sea salt is preferred. If you can't find "petite diced tomatoes," as called for in some recipes, regular diced tomatoes are fine. I simply prefer the flavor and appearance of the smaller-cut tomatoes that are now available in supermarkets. When chopped scallions are listed, it refers to both the white and green parts.

When specific can or jar sizes are called for, these sizes are based on what is available in my local store. If your store carries 15-ounce canned beans and the recipe calls for a 16-ounce can, for example, it's perfectly fine to go with the size found in your store. A small size differential either way will not adversely affect the recipes.

a word about vegetables

While I believe in using as much fresh organic, preferably locally grown, produce as possible, I am also a realist. Sometimes fresh organic produce is not available in the varieties we need, is astronomically priced, or is out of season. Also, if you limit your shopping to once a week, you may not be able to buy enough fresh produce to last that long.

The solution is to buy some frozen vegetables that can be incorporated into your meals later in the week. Frozen veggies are already prepped and easy to use. Since they are frozen when they are fresh, they can be fresher than the "fresh" veggies in your supermarket, which may have been picked early and shipped long distances. They're also economical, cook quickly, and can help you get through the week making fast and healthy meals.

Among my favorite frozen vegetables are artichoke hearts, baby green peas, bell pepper strips, chopped spinach, edamame, brussels sprouts, and corn kernels. Mixed-vegetable medleys can come in handy as well. I also use certain canned vegetables, most notably tomatoes and tomato products, artichoke hearts, pumpkin, corn, and, of course, canned beans of all kinds, from chickpeas to pintos.

Today's fresh vegetables are not without their own conveniences. Consider the wide variety of prewashed and prepared salad mixes from baby spinach to mixed field greens to crunchy romaine. Just open the bag and toss in a bowl. If you use bottled dressings, your salad is ready in seconds. How's that for fast food? Also convenient are baby carrots, because they can be used without having to be peeled. Like bagged lettuces, bagged shredded cabbage is available, primarily for coleslaw, but it's also ideal for cooking when recipes call for shredded cabbage.

For those in a real time-crunch, there are even presliced mushrooms, fresh chopped onions, and bags of fresh stir-fry vegetables.

Many of the recipes call for "½ cup chopped onion," for example, instead of "1 small onion, chopped." This allows you the choice of buying ingredients that are already chopped or buying them whole to chop yourself.

Generally, you can assume that vegetables listed in the recipes are trimmed, washed, scrubbed, or peeled unless otherwise noted.

about meat and dairy alternatives

Protein-rich foods such as beans and tofu are popular plant-based alternatives to meat. In addition to these mainstays, there is a wide variety of prepared vegetarian protein options such as veggie burgers, sausages, and burger "crumbles." These products can be used to replace meat in recipes that normally call for meat, or enjoyed in interesting new ways. There are also numerous soy-based products such as soy milk, soy mayonnaise, and soy cheeses available to replace dairy products. These plant-based options provide good sources of protein and other nutrients, are low in fat, contain no cholesterol, and can be used to make healthful well-balanced meals. Most of these products are available in well-stocked supermarkets or natural food stores.

built for speed— kitchen equipment

Outfitting a kitchen is largely a combination of lifestyle, budget, and personal preferences. I know some people who have cramped kitchens and limited equipment who cook fabulous meals and others who have giant kitchens equipped with every conceivable gadget who eat most of their meals in restaurants. I think cooking is more about the cook and the ingredients than the equipment, although you should have the best equipment you can for your budget.

It is not my purpose here to recommend cast iron over copper or Le Creuset over Calphalon. Suffice it to say that every kitchen needs at least one pot big enough to boil pasta and make a large quantity of vegetable stock, and a couple of smaller saucepans, including one with a steamer insert for steaming vegetables. Heavy-bottomed skillets ranging in size from 8 inches to 16 inches in diameter are a must. At least one skillet should have a nonstick surface. All pots and skillets should have lids that fit well.

Most people know that every kitchen needs mixing bowls, measuring cups, a colander, and a can opener. What some people may not know is which tools make cooking easier and quicker, and so I provide the following list of equipment that I have found to be "built for speed."

- **Knives:** If I could have only three knives in my possession, they would be a paring knife for peeling and trimming; a long serrated knife for slicing bread, tomatoes, and the like; and a good chef's knife for virtually everything else. Buy the best-quality knives you can afford and keep them sharp. You can chop more quickly and safely with sharp knives than dull ones.

- **Cutting boards:** A few good cutting boards in various sizes are essential to a "quick-fix" kitchen. If you just have one tiny board the size of a postage stamp, it will slow you down considerably. It's best to have at least two boards in case you need to chop more than one item, so you don't get slowed down by having to stop and wash the cutting board. I prefer polypropylene boards because they're easy to clean, nonporous, and don't dull knives.

- **Food processor:** A food processor is essential for making pesto, pureeing vegetables, chopping nuts, and making bread crumbs. It is also great for making

pie dough, chopping vegetables, and numerous other mixing and chopping tasks. The trick is knowing when it will be faster to cut, whisk, or chop by hand, and that can usually be determined by the quantity of food involved. In addition to a large-capacity processor, some people also have a smaller model that they use for smaller tasks.

- **Blender:** For the longest time, I got along with just a food processor and no blender. Then I got a high-powered blender, and my cooking habits changed. I now use both blender and food processor for different purposes. The blender is reserved for smoothies, sauces, soups, and anything I want to make super smooth and creamy very quickly. Another plus of having both a food processor and a blender in play is that when making multiple recipes, I can often avoid stopping to wash out one or the other, since I can easily use them both.

- **Immersion blender:** The advantage of the immersion blender is that it is easier to clean than the regular blender and it saves the time of pouring your recipe into a blender container, since you can blend the food right in the bowl or pot that it's already in. It's especially handy for pureeing soup right in the pot.

- **Box grater:** This versatile tool can be used instead of the food processor when you have a small amount of anything from citrus zest to cabbage that needs grating or shredding. For extra-small jobs, use a microplane grater.

- **Mandoline:** I like to use a mandoline when I need very thin slices very fast. Sure, you can always slice ingredients with a knife or even the slicing attachment of a food processor, but this handy gadget lets you cut uniform slices, from thick to paper-thin, with ease and swiftness. Note: The plastic Benriner slicer is a smaller version of the stainless steel mandoline and is much less expensive. It works great and is a good choice for the budget-minded.

- **Salad spinner:** By far the easiest and quickest way to dry your salad greens after washing them. No more laying out individual lettuce leaves to dry on paper towels. This thing really works great to get every drop of water off your lettuce, leaving it crisp and ready for your salad.

- **Vegetable peeler:** Essential for peeling carrots, potatoes, cucumbers, etc. It's quick, easy, and very low-tech, but indispensable.

making the most of the microwave

While I'd never use my microwave to actually cook dinner, I have found it to be quite useful in getting dinner on the table. It's great for wilting fresh spinach and softening hard winter squashes to make them easier to cut. I also use the microwave when I need just a small amount of melted margarine, chocolate, or hot water. It's also useful at dinnertime when you're busy preparing multiple dishes and you can use the microwave to prevent a logjam by reheating a dish that was prepared in advance.

slow-cooking in a fast-food world

It may sound odd to suggest that a recipe that takes up to eight hours to cook can be considered "fast food," but here's the reasoning:

As any slow-cooker aficionado will tell you, cooking in a slow cooker has numerous benefits. Once you spend a few minutes assembling and preparing the ingredients, everything goes into the cooker, which spends the day gently cooking your meal. The safe, slow cooking allows you to leave it unattended, so you can do other things—even leave the house—while dinner cooks. Add to that the deep, rich flavor that comes from slow-cooking, and it's easy to see why this cooking method is so popular. Since it is conceivable that you can literally sit down to eat dinner the minute you arrive home, I believe that slow-cooker recipes deserve a chapter in a "quick-fix" book.

I used the same reasoning for the chapter on oven-baked recipes. While most of those recipes take less than an hour to bake, they can be assembled in just a few minutes. One of the main advantages of oven-baked foods is that you can assemble them ahead of time and then bake them when you need them. Plus, since you bake and serve in the same vessel, there's no messy cleanup to worry about.

In terms of convenience and variety, then, it becomes clear how some recipes that take longer to cook can actually be more convenient to prepare.

cooking for a crowd: panic-free parties

Entertaining doesn't need to be stressful or fussy. There are lots of "quick-fix" ways to cook for a crowd without pushing the panic button. Here are some ideas:

Plan an easy menu. Sit-down dinners are more work than buffets, so unless it's for a very small group, food that can be set out for people to help themselves is a good choice.

Depending on the occasion, you can go the snack route and just serve a variety of chips, crackers, dips, and cut fruits and veggies. You could add one hot dish, such as a stew or chili, with bread and a salad.

When choosing hot items, plan for something that can be made ahead and reheated at serving time.

Incorporate some prepared items in your menu, such as store-bought hummus, vegetable sushi, focaccia, or a special dessert.

Don't leave too much work for the last minute. Be sure all cleaning is done ahead of time, including the kitchen. If you start with a clean kitchen and your food is all prepped, it's smooth sailing from there. Just dish it up and serve.

convenience foods—store-bought or homemade

Whether planning ahead means keeping several containers of homemade vegetable broth in the freezer or buying a few cans for the cupboard, the important thing is to keep essential ingredients on hand to prevent time-wasting extra shopping trips for one or two ingredients.

There are many recipes in this book that call for ingredients that can be either made from scratch or purchased at the store. If you opt for the store-bought, then all you need to do is stock your pantry with a few basic items. If you prefer to go the homemade route, then you'll probably need the following recipes at one point or another.

Below are the recipes and cooking instructions for some of the items frequently called for in this book. I've also included descriptions of the store-bought versions of these ingredients that can be found at well-stocked supermarkets and natural food stores.

recipes are vegan

The recipes in this book are pure vegetarian (vegan), which means that they contain no animal ingredients whatsoever. This is good news for people who are lactose-intolerant or watching their cholesterol.

vegetable broth

makes about 8 cups

This basic vegetable broth can be cooled and frozen in several containers so you can defrost exactly what you need for a recipe. As in all recipes, be sure to scrub and wash all vegetables well before using.

2 tablespoons extra-virgin olive oil
2 onions, coarsely chopped
3 carrots, coarsely chopped
2 potatoes, quartered
3 celery ribs, including leaves, chopped
4 cloves garlic, crushed

12 cups water
2 tablespoons tamari
1 cup coarsely chopped fresh parsley
2 bay leaves
½ teaspoon salt
½ teaspoon black peppercorns

Heat the oil in a large stockpot over medium heat. Add the onions, carrots, potatoes, celery, and garlic. Cover and cook until slightly softened, about 5 minutes. Add the water, tamari, parsley, bay leaves, salt, and peppercorns. Bring to a boil, then decrease the heat to medium-low and simmer, uncovered, for 1 hour to reduce the liquid and bring out the flavors of the vegetables.

Strain the liquid through a fine-mesh sieve into another pot, pressing the juices out of the vegetables with the back of a large spoon. The broth is now ready to use. For a stronger broth, bring the broth back to a boil, and reduce the volume by one-quarter. Tightly covered, this broth keeps well in the refrigerator for up to 4 days and, portioned, in the freezer for up to 3 months.

note: Commercial vegetable broth is available in cans and aseptic cartons. The strength and flavor of the broth varies greatly by brand, so be sure to find one you like. In addition to these full-strength broths, you can buy vegetable bouillon cubes and powdered vegetable base that can be turned into a broth with the addition of boiling water.

It is important to note that because of the wide range of saltiness of the different broths, including homemade ones, many of the recipes in this book call for salt to be added "to taste" so that you can use more or less depending on the saltiness of the broth used.

Here's an easy guide to "quick-fix" vegetable broth:
• Canned vegetable broth
• Vegetable broth in aseptic cartons
• Vegetable bouillon cubes
• Powdered vegetable base

As with any packaged food, check the ingredients for additives, and buy the healthiest one. When using broths, taste them for strength, since some have a stronger flavor than others that may encroach on the flavor of your finished dish. For a milder broth, dilute the canned broth with water, by half. For example, if a recipe calls for 4 cups of broth, you can use one can of broth (approximately 2 cups) plus 2 cups of water. This is also more economical.

mushroom gravy

makes about 2 cups

This all-purpose brown sauce can be used any time you need a brown gravy. It is especially good with seitan or in potpies and similar dishes. While the sauce could also be made without the miso, I think it adds a rich depth of flavor that would otherwise not be there. If you want a chunky rather than smooth sauce, scoop out some of the cooked mushrooms before pureeing the gravy and then stir them back in to heat through.

1 tablespoon extra-virgin olive oil
¼ cup chopped onion
1 clove garlic, minced
2 cups sliced mushrooms
2 tablespoons tamari
½ teaspoon dried thyme
1½ cups water

1½ tablespoons cornstarch dissolved in 3 tablespoons water
1 tablespoon miso paste (optional)
Freshly ground black pepper
½ teaspoon gravy browning liquid, such as Kitchen Bouquet or GravyMaster (optional)

Heat the oil in a saucepan over medium heat. Add the onion and garlic. Cover and cook until softened, about 5 minutes. Stir in the mushrooms, cover, and cook 2 minutes more.

Stir in the tamari, thyme, and water, and bring to a boil. Add the cornstarch mixture and cook, stirring, until thickened, 2 to 3 minutes. Decrease the heat to low and stir in the miso paste and pepper to taste.

Pour the gravy mixture into a blender or food processor and puree until smooth. Return to the saucepan and taste to adjust the seasonings before serving, reheating as necessary. Do not boil. For a richer brown color, stir in up to ½ teaspoon of browning liquid. Tightly covered, this sauce keeps well in the refrigerator for up to 4 days and in the freezer for up to 3 months.

note: Many of the recipes in this book call for mushroom gravy. You can make your own using the recipe above or buy a commercial brand. It's important to check the label when buying prepared gravy, since some contain animal products. Two products that contain no animal ingredients are Campbell's mushroom gravy, sold in 10.5-ounce cans in many supermarkets, and Tofurky gravy, which is sold in the frozen section of natural food stores in 14-ounce plastic containers. Packets of vegetarian gravy mixes are also available in natural food stores and some supermarkets.

basil pesto

makes about 1 cup

This basic pesto recipe can be altered to suit your tastes. I like to make my pesto "poor man's" style (without cheese), which allows it to be frozen in small containers. Be sure to cover with a layer of olive oil to help it retain its color.

3 to 4 cloves garlic, crushed
½ cup pine nuts
1 teaspoon salt

3 cups firmly packed fresh basil leaves
½ cup extra-virgin olive oil

In a food processor, combine the garlic, pine nuts, and salt and process until well ground. Add the basil and process until finely minced. Add the oil and process until smooth.

The pesto is now ready to use. If not using immediately, pour a thin layer of olive oil on top of the pesto, cover tightly, and refrigerate until ready to use. Properly stored, it will keep in the refrigerator for up to 1 week and in the freezer for up to 3 months.

note: Commercially made pesto can be found in small jars in most supermarkets near the pastas and pasta sauces. Vegans take note that most commercial pesto contains dairy products.

tapenade

makes about 1 cup

Use this recipe to make either black or green olive tapenade. While it's a good idea to keep bottled tapenade on hand for emergencies, making your own is economical and easy, especially when you begin with pitted olives. If pitted olives are unavailable, it will take a few extra minutes to pit them. Another plus of making your own tapenade is the ability to control the amount of garlic and capers to your own taste.

1 clove garlic
¾ cup pitted black or green olives
1 tablespoon capers, drained and rinsed

3 tablespoons chopped fresh parsley
⅛ teaspoon freshly ground black pepper
3 tablespoons extra-virgin olive oil

Mince the garlic in a food processor. Add the olives, capers, parsley, and pepper and process until well chopped. Add the olive oil and pulse to a coarse paste. Taste to adjust the seasonings. Refrigerated in a tightly covered container, tapenade keeps well for up to 1 week.

note: Tapenade is now widely available in supermarkets and gourmet specialty shops. They can range from the traditional black olive tapenade and green olive tapenade to even those flavored with sun-dried tomatoes, figs, and other ingredients. Commercially made tapenade can be expensive, but it is very convenient and certainly worth keeping on hand.

pie dough

makes enough for 2 crusts

This recipe makes enough for one double-crust pie or two single-crust pies. Make ahead and freeze the flattened dough for when you need it. Then simply defrost and roll out.

2 cups unbleached all-purpose flour
1 teaspoon salt

⅔ cup nonhydrogenated margarine, cut into small pieces (try Earth Balance brand)
¼ cup ice water, plus additional as needed

Combine the flour and salt in a food processor. Blend in the margarine with short pulses until the mixture becomes crumbly. With the machine running, add the water through the feed tube and blend until the dough just starts to hold together. Transfer the dough to a work surface, divide it in half, and flatten to form two disks. Wrap the dough in plastic wrap and refrigerate for 30 minutes. Tightly wrapped, the dough keeps well in the freezer for up to 3 months.

note: Frozen piecrusts (in aluminum pie plates) are available in supermarkets and natural food stores. Be sure to read the label carefully, since some brands may contain lard.

roasted bell peppers

Bell peppers can be roasted directly over the gas flame on your stove top by holding the pepper over the flame with tongs and turning it frequently to allow the skin to blister and blacken. Whole peppers can also be roasted on a grill, turning frequently until charred, or you can roast them in the oven or under a broiler. To roast peppers in the oven, put the peppers directly on the oven rack and roast until blistered and charred.

When the peppers are charred, close them inside a paper or plastic bag. Allow to cool for 10 minutes, then remove the peppers from the bag and remove the skins. Cut out the stem and slice the peppers open. Remove the core and seeds and cut into pieces. If not using right away, pour a thin layer of olive oil over the peppers and refrigerate in a tightly covered container. They will keep well for up to 1 week.

note: Bottled roasted red bell peppers are sold in supermarkets in 6-ounce and 12-ounce jars, packed in oil.

toasted nuts and seeds

Nuts can be toasted in two ways—either on top of the stove in a dry skillet, or in the oven on a baking pan. To toast nuts in the oven, preheat the oven to 350°F. Place the nuts in a single layer in a small, shallow baking pan. Toast, stirring occasionally, until very lightly browned and fragrant, 2 to 8 minutes, depending on the type of nut. Pine nuts, sliced almonds, and sesame seeds, for example, begin to brown very quickly, whereas heartier nuts such as walnuts and pecans take longer. Remove the toasted nuts from the oven and allow to cool completely.

To toast nuts on the stove top, place them in a dry small skillet over medium heat and toast them, stirring or shaking the pan occasionally, until lightly browned, 1 to 5 minutes, depending on the nut. Be careful not to burn them. Allow to cool completely.

Alternately, you can also toast nuts in a toaster oven. Keep a close watch on them so they don't burn, as they can brown rather quickly.

If not using right away, allow the nuts to cool completely before storing. If tightly wrapped, toasted nuts can be kept refrigerated or frozen for several weeks.

note: Depending on the variety of nut, you may or may not find them already toasted. In the case of the toasted nuts used in this book, such as sliced or slivered almonds, pine nuts, and walnuts, these are usually sold raw.

appetizers

Because hors d'oeuvres and other appetizers have a reputation for being fussy and time-consuming, they're often reserved for company or special occasions. But, as the recipes in this chapter illustrate, all appetizers are not created equal. These recipes are designed to impress without stress and are ideal for occasions when there's no time to fuss, but you want it to seem like you did.

Nothing makes guests feel special like serving a tasty bite before dinner, and these tempting tidbits are just the ticket. When you enlist the aid of convenient ingredients such as puff pastry, tortillas, and tapenade, a fabulous appetizer is just minutes away. But why wait for company? These recipes are so easy to prepare, you may want to make them for yourself, too. Another plus—many of these recipes would be great for lunch or a light supper. For example, the Harissa-Spiced White Bean Dip, the Green Onion Hummus with Lime, and the Artichoke Dip with a Twist all make great spreads for wraps or sandwiches. Add a fresh green salad to the Polenta with Two-Tomato Topping, the Spinach and Sun-Dried Tomato Quesadillas, or the Tomato and Olive Bruschetta, and you have a satisfying meal.

guacamole roll-ups

serves 4

This tasty appetizer contains the luscious flavors of avocado, lime, and your favorite salsa, all rolled up in a soft flour tortilla, with a few shreds of lettuce for crunch. They're also great for lunch—I especially like making them with whole wheat tortillas.

2 ripe Hass avocados
½ cup tomato salsa
Juice of 1 lime

Salt and freshly ground black pepper
4 large flour tortillas, warmed
1 cup finely shredded romaine lettuce

Halve and pit the avocados. Scoop out the flesh with a spoon and place it in a bowl. Add the salsa and lime juice and mash together to blend. Season with salt and pepper to taste.

Place the tortillas on a flat work surface and spread about ¼ cup of the guacamole mixture across each tortilla. Sprinkle with the shredded romaine. Roll up the tortillas, cut into 1-inch slices, and stand on end. Serve at once.

quicker fix

Instead of making your own guacamole, use ready-made guacamole found in the refrigerated produce section of your supermarket.

pastry-wrapped stuffed olives

makes 16 to 20

Crunchy almonds or fiery jalapeños replace the pits in these pastry-enrobed olives. Some might call this one "fussy," but with only two ingredients that pack a dramatic flavor punch, I consider the fuss factor negligible. If you love the combination of olives and pastry as much as I do, you'll definitely agree. If you can't find the large green olives already stuffed with almonds or jalapeños, you can buy large pitted green olives and stuff your own. If this is the only hors d'oeuvre you're serving, make sure your guests are card-carrying olive lovers. And if you make some of each kind, be sure to separate the almond-filled from the jalapeño-filled—unless your guests enjoy surprises.

1 frozen deep-dish piecrust, thawed
16 to 20 almond- or jalapeño-stuffed green olives

Preheat the oven to 400°F. Roll out the thawed pastry crust. Use a sharp knife or a pizza cutter to divide the pastry into 16 to 20 pieces about 2 inches square. (You will need to patch the rounded end scraps together to make a few of the pieces.)

Lightly flour your hands to keep the pastry from sticking to them. Press 1 square of the pastry around each olive to enclose completely, molding with your hands as needed to shape into smooth ovoids. Place on a greased baking sheet. Refrigerate for about 10 minutes to firm up or until ready to use. Bake until golden brown, about 15 minutes. Serve warm or at room temperature.

note: These can be made ahead and stored at room temperature. To serve, crisp in a preheated 400°F oven for 2 to 3 minutes.

ingredient alert

Be sure to check the ingredients on the piecrust—some brands contain lard.

mango lettuce wraps

serves 4

This recipe was inspired by a refreshing and simple appetizer I enjoyed at Teapot, a fabulous vegan restaurant in Seattle. My version is embellished with additional ingredients to add contrasting textures and flavors, but you could also use only the mango on the lettuce, if you prefer. This one works best as a seated appetizer, although smaller versions can be made if you'd like to serve them on a buffet or pass them on a tray.

2 tablespoons freshly squeezed lime juice
1 tablespoon pure maple syrup or agave syrup
2 or 3 red radishes
1 teaspoon minced fresh chives

1 very ripe mango, peeled, halved, and pitted
4 large or 8 small Boston lettuce leaves
Freshly ground black pepper
Chopped peanuts or pistachios, for garnish

In a small bowl combine the lime juice and maple syrup until well blended. Set aside.

Cut the radishes into thin matchstick julienne strips and add to the bowl with the lime sauce. Add the chives and toss gently to coat.

Cut the mango halves lengthwise into thin slices. Place a few slices of the mango on each lettuce leaf and arrange on a platter or individual plates. Top with the radish mixture and a few grinds of black pepper. Garnish with chopped nuts and serve.

herbed mushroom crostini

serves 6

Smaller and more delicate than bruschetta, crostini traditionally have more genteel toppings than the bolder bruschetta. A French baguette is the ideal size bread to make crostini.

1 tablespoon extra-virgin olive oil, plus
    additional for brushing the bread
½ baguette loaf, cut crosswise into 12 slices,
    about ½ inch thick
1 clove garlic, minced
8 ounces mushrooms, finely chopped

¼ teaspoon dried basil
¼ teaspoon dried marjoram
¼ teaspoon dried savory
Salt and freshly ground black pepper
1 tablespoon minced fresh parsley

Preheat the broiler or grill. Lightly brush olive oil onto both sides of the bread slices and place on a baking sheet.

Heat the 1 tablespoon olive oil in a large skillet over medium heat. Add the garlic and cook until fragrant, about 1 minute. Stir in the mushrooms, basil, marjoram, and savory. Season to taste with salt and pepper. Cook, stirring occasionally, until the mushrooms are soft, 5 to 7 minutes. Stir in the parsley. Keep warm while you toast the bread.

Broil or grill the bread until golden brown, being careful not to burn it. Spoon the hot mushroom mixture over the toasted bread. Serve hot.

tomato and olive bruschetta

serves 4 to 6

Bruschetta is the bigger, more rustic cousin of the crostini. While French baguettes make ideal crostini bread, the larger Italian loaves are perfect for bruschetta. The bread is traditionally grilled, but it can be broiled or toasted as well.

2 large ripe tomatoes, chopped
½ cup pitted Kalamata olives, chopped
1 tablespoon minced fresh parsley or basil
Salt and freshly ground black pepper

4 to 6 (about ¾-inch thick) slices good Italian bread
Extra-virgin olive oil, for brushing the bread
1 or 2 cloves garlic, halved

Preheat the grill or broiler. In a bowl, combine the tomatoes, olives, parsley, and salt and pepper to taste. Set aside.

Lightly brush both sides of the bread slices with olive oil and grill or broil the bread until lightly browned. Be careful not to burn it.

Rub one side of each slice of the toasted bread with the garlic. To serve, top each piece of bread with a spoonful of topping or serve the topping in a bowl surrounded by the toasted bread, for guests to serve themselves.

spinach and sun-dried tomato quesadillas

serves 4

Baby spinach comes already washed and ready to add its great flavor and nutrients to your meals. In this recipe, spinach combines with sun-dried tomatoes and a heart-healthy cream cheese to make yummy and slightly chic quesadillas. To serve as pickup appetizers, cut the quesadillas into small wedges and arrange on a platter.

1 (10-ounce) package fresh baby spinach
2 tablespoons water
1 cup nonhydrogenated soy cream cheese
½ cup minced oil-packed sun-dried tomatoes

Salt and freshly ground black pepper
4 large flour tortillas
Extra-virgin olive oil, for oiling skillet

Place the spinach in a glass bowl with the water. Cover and microwave until wilted, about 3 minutes. Allow to cool, remove from the bowl, and squeeze out any liquid. Chop well and set aside.

In a bowl, combine the soy cream cheese, tomatoes, chopped spinach, and salt and pepper to taste. Mix well.

Divide the mixture among the tortillas, spreading the mixture onto one-half of each of them. Fold the tortillas over, pressing gently to seal in the filling.

Heat a large lightly oiled skillet over medium heat. Place one or two of the quesadillas in the pan and cook until warmed and slightly browned, about 5 minutes per side. Repeat with the remaining quesadillas. To serve, cut each quesadilla into 4 wedges and arrange on a platter or tray.

variations

Use shredded soy mozzarella instead of the cream cheese or make the quesadillas with shredded soy Cheddar cheese and a small can of drained mild green chiles.

health note

This recipe calls for nonhydrogenated soy cream cheese—a delicious, heart-healthy product widely available at natural food stores. No cholesterol, no trans-fatty acids, but great flavor. What more could you want from a cream cheese?

polenta with two-tomato topping

serves 4

To keep this recipe in the "quick-fix" category, it calls for cooked polenta, which can be found two different ways, depending on the supermarket. In the produce section, polenta is sold in the refrigerated case. There is also a shelf-stable cooked polenta that can be found in the dried pasta section of many supermarkets. Depending on which you buy, the polenta will be shaped like a log or a rectangle. Once you slice the polenta, you can further cut the slices into bite-sized pieces if passing on a tray or placing on a buffet, or leave the slices larger if plating for individual servings.

3 to 4 large ripe yellow tomatoes, chopped
½ cup chopped oil-packed sun-dried tomatoes
¼ cup extra-virgin olive oil
1 tablespoon white wine vinegar

2 tablespoons minced fresh basil or parsley
Salt and freshly ground black pepper
1 (16-ounce) package precooked polenta, cut into ½-inch slices

In a bowl, combine the fresh and dried tomatoes with 2 tablespoons of the oil, the vinegar, the basil, and salt and pepper to taste. Toss gently to combine. Set aside while you cook the polenta.

Heat the remaining 2 tablespoons of olive oil in a large skillet over medium heat. Add the polenta slices and cook until browned on both sides, about 3 minutes per side.

To serve, top the polenta slices with the tomato mixture and arrange on a platter.

note: While I love the striking color contrast of the fresh yellow tomatoes and the red sun-dried tomatoes, yellow tomatoes may not always be available. In that case, you can use fresh red tomatoes for equally delicious, if monochromatic, results.

note, too: If you prefer to cook your polenta from scratch, by all means do so. Just prepare it well ahead of time, so it has time to chill for several hours before proceeding with the recipe.

tapenade pastry twists

makes about 24

Frozen puff pastry is the secret behind these opulent treats. Plan ahead when using puff pastry because it takes 30 minutes to thaw. Although tapenade is evocative of olives, the name references the capers that are also present.

1 sheet frozen puff pastry, thawed
1 cup black olive tapenade (page 18)

Preheat the oven to 400°F. Unfold the thawed pastry onto a lightly floured surface. Use a rolling pin to roll out the pastry into a thin rectangle. Cut in half lengthwise. Spread the tapenade on one of the pastry halves. Place the remaining pastry half over the one with the tapenade. Roll gently with the rolling pin to seal. Use a sharp knife or a pizza wheel to cut crosswise into ½-inch strips. Twist the strips and place on a greased baking sheet, about 2 inches apart. Press down the ends of each pastry twist so it remains twisted.

Bake until golden brown, about 10 minutes. Serve warm or at room temperature.

quicker fix

Instead of making your own, buy a commercially prepared tapenade at the supermarket.

green onion hummus with lime

makes about 2 cups

Over the last few years, hummus has become ubiquitous at parties, on menus, and in cookbooks. And with good reason—it's easy to make, tastes great, and is healthful and versatile to boot. Supermarkets now sell containers of the popular chickpea and tahini dip in a variety of flavors. No collection of quick and easy vegetarian appetizers would be complete without a hummus recipe. So here's my latest take on an old favorite—a refreshing lime and green onion version of the classic.

2 to 3 scallions (green onions), coarsely chopped
1 (16-ounce) can chickpeas, drained and rinsed
¼ cup tahini (sesame paste)

2½ tablespoons freshly squeezed lime juice
½ teaspoon salt
⅛ teaspoon cayenne
2 tablespoons extra-virgin olive oil
Paprika, for garnish

In a food processor, process the scallions until finely minced. Add the chickpeas and tahini and process until smooth. Add the lime juice, salt, and cayenne and process until well combined.

With the machine running, slowly stream in the oil and process until smooth. Taste to adjust the seasonings. Transfer to a bowl and sprinkle with paprika.

note: You can serve the hummus right away or cover and refrigerate for an hour or two, which will allow the flavors to intensify.

variation

For a more traditional hummus, swap the scallions and lime juice for garlic cloves and lemon juice in the same proportions.

serving suggestion

Serve with your favorite crackers or Pita Triangles (page 39).

artichoke dip with a twist

serves 8

A twist of lemon is not the only twist in this redo of an old-time favorite. Another is the protein-rich white beans that are used to replace the artery-clogging mayonnaise, making this a dip that is tasty and good for you, too. Now that's a twist.

2 (9-ounce) packages frozen artichoke
　　hearts
1 cup canned Great Northern beans or other
　　white beans, drained and rinsed
¼ cup grated soy Parmesan cheese
2 tablespoons extra-virgin olive oil
1 tablespoon freshly squeezed lemon juice

½ teaspoon Tabasco
Salt
¼ cup dry bread crumbs
1 (¼ by 2-inch) piece lemon peel
1 tablespoon black sesame seeds or
　　chopped fresh parsley

Preheat the oven to 350°F. Cook the artichokes according to package directions. Drain well, pat dry, then coarsely chop the artichoke hearts and set aside.

In a food processor, combine the beans, soy Parmesan, 1 tablespoon of the olive oil, the lemon juice, and Tabasco. Process until well blended. Add the chopped artichokes and process to mix well. Season with salt to taste.

Transfer the artichoke mixture to a lightly oiled 8-inch baking dish. Top with the bread crumbs, drizzle with the remaining 1 tablespoon olive oil, and bake until hot, about 20 minutes. Garnish with the twist of lemon peel and the sesame seeds or parsley.

quicker fix

Canned artichoke hearts may be used instead of frozen. Look for the ones packed in water, not the marinated kind. Drain well and pat dry before using.

variation

Besides a twist of lemon, you can fold one of the following into the dip for an additional color and flavor nuance: chopped sun-dried tomatoes, black olives, pimiento, or roasted red bell peppers.

green olive–edamame dip

makes about 1½ cups

The piquancy of the green olives combines with the subtly sweet creaminess of edamame for a delicious and unusual dip that will have guests doing a double take: To look at it, one might mistake it for guacamole, but one taste will tell you otherwise. Starting with shelled edamame and pitted olives keeps this recipe especially speedy.

1 cup fresh or frozen shelled edamame
½ cup pitted green olives
½ teaspoon minced garlic

Salt and freshly ground black pepper
2 tablespoons chopped tomato

Cook the edamame in salted boiling water until soft, about 10 minutes. Drain, reserving some of the hot cooking liquid. Puree the edamame in a food processor, adding about ¼ cup of the hot cooking liquid for a smooth texture. Add the olives and garlic and process until smooth and well blended. Taste for seasoning, adding salt and pepper if needed. Transfer to a bowl and garnish with the tomato.

serving suggestion

Serve with crudités, crackers, or other dippers.

red pepper and walnut spread

makes about 2 cups

This spread was inspired by an appetizer called muhammara found in Middle Eastern countries such as Syria and Turkey. In the original, roasted red bell peppers and walnuts are flavored with pomegranate syrup. If you have pomegranate syrup on hand, you can use it to replace the maple syrup in this recipe.

½ cup chopped walnut pieces
1 slice white bread, torn into pieces, or ½ cup dry bread crumbs
1 (12-ounce) jar roasted red bell peppers, drained and coarsely chopped
Juice of 1 lemon
1 teaspoon balsamic vinegar
1 tablespoon pure maple syrup

½ teaspoon chili paste, or to taste
½ teaspoon salt
¼ teaspoon ground cumin
1 tablespoon extra-virgin olive oil, plus additional as needed
Chopped fresh parsley or walnut pieces, for garnish

In a food processor, process the walnuts and bread until finely ground. Add the roasted red peppers, lemon juice, vinegar, maple syrup, and chili paste, and blend until smooth. Season with the salt and cumin. Add the olive oil and blend until smooth. Taste and adjust the seasonings, and add more oil if needed for consistency. Place in a bowl and garnish with chopped parsley or walnuts.

note: If not using right away, cover and refrigerate.

serving suggestion

Serve with Pita Triangles (page 39), crackers, or cut-up vegetables.

fast and fresh
spinach-edamame dip

makes about 1½ cups

This is a great way to combine two ready-to-use produce staples—fresh baby spinach and fresh or frozen shelled edamame. Serve with raw vegetable dippers or your favorite crackers.

1 cup fresh or frozen shelled edamame
1 (10-ounce) package fresh baby spinach
2 tablespoons water
1 (4-ounce) can diced mild green chiles, drained

3 scallions, chopped
Juice of 1 lemon
½ teaspoon salt
Cayenne

Cook the edamame in salted boiling water until soft, about 10 minutes. Drain the edamame and set aside. Place the spinach in a glass bowl with the water. Cover and microwave until wilted, about 3 minutes. Allow to cool, remove from the bowl, and squeeze out any liquid. Set aside.

In a food processor, puree the edamame until smooth. Add the wilted spinach, chiles, scallions, lemon juice, salt, and cayenne to taste. Process until well blended. Transfer to a bowl.

note: The dip can be eaten right away, but its flavor intensifies if covered and refrigerated for at least 1 hour before serving.

variation

For a creamier consistency, add 1 tablespoon of soy mayonnaise to the mixture.

harissa-spiced white bean dip

makes about 1½ cups

Don't let its mild-mannered appearance fool you—this bean dip is one hot number thanks to the addition of fiery harissa (page 176), a Tunisian sauce made with hot chiles, garlic, and spices. For a tamer version, omit or cut back on the harissa sauce. Prepared harissa is also available in well-stocked supermarkets and specialty grocers.

1 clove garlic, crushed
1 (16-ounce) can Great Northern beans or
    other white beans, drained and rinsed
2 tablespoons tahini (sesame paste)
1 tablespoon freshly squeezed lemon juice,
    plus additional to taste

1½ teaspoons harissa sauce (page 176),
    or to taste
Salt and freshly ground black pepper
1 tablespoon finely minced scallions

Mince the garlic in a blender or food processor. Add the remaining ingredients except the scallions and process until smooth. Taste and adjust the seasonings. Transfer to a bowl and garnish with minced scallions sprinkled on top.

note: You can serve this dip as soon as it is made, or cover it and refrigerate for an hour or two to allow the flavors to intensify.

serving suggestion

This dip is especially good served with Pita Triangles (page 39).

pita triangles

makes 64

You can save time and buy pita chips at the store instead of making them, but homemade ones taste fresher and are more economical. In addition to or instead of salt and pepper, you can season the pita triangles with dried herbs, sesame seeds, or poppy seeds.

4 (7-inch) pita bread rounds
Extra-virgin olive oil, for brushing the pita
    bread

Salt and freshly ground black pepper

Preheat the oven to 350°F. Use a small serrated knife to carefully split each pita round into 2 circles. Brush or drizzle a small amount of olive oil onto the inner surface of the pita bread.

Cut the pita circles into eighths to make 64 triangles. Arrange the pita on a cookie sheet in a single layer. Sprinkle with salt and pepper.

Bake until golden brown, about 10 minutes. Serve warm or allow to cool.

note: Pita triangles taste best when eaten on the day they are made but will keep well for a day or two when stored at room temperature in a tightly sealed container. Just be sure to allow to cool completely before storing.

serving suggestions

Serve pita triangles as an accompaniment to any of the dips in this chapter. They are especially suited to accompany the Harissa-Spiced White Bean Dip, the Red Pepper and Walnut Spread, and the Green Onion Hummus with Lime.

soups

Homemade soups are often associated with time-consuming prep and even longer cooking time. But that doesn't mean you have to settle for less. Somewhere between a slow-simmering potage and canned soup is a selection of fast and thrifty homemade soups for every season that taste like they took hours instead of minutes to prepare.

Whichever of these satisfying soups you choose, from the hearty Barley and Bean Soup with Rainbow Chard to the refreshing Chilled Cucumber Avocado Soup, they are all ready to eat, start to finish, in 30 minutes or less.

One secret to most quick soups is having vegetable broth waiting in the wings. This broth can be homemade, canned or packaged, or made on the spot with powdered vegetable base or vegetarian bouillon cubes (see Note, page 15).

Another secret to making speedy soups is using quick-cooking vegetables and other convenient ingredients such as canned beans and frozen or precut vegetables. Add the right seasonings to suit your taste and bring out the flavor of the ingredients, and you'll have a tasty, full-bodied soup in no time.

creamy tortilla soup

serves 4

This silky rich soup is creamy with a refreshing note of lime. Choose from mild, medium, or hot salsa to determine the heat intensity of the soup.

1 tablespoon extra-virgin olive oil, plus
  additional for brushing the tortillas
2 cloves garlic, chopped
1½ cups tomato salsa
4 cups vegetable broth (page 15)

2 ripe Hass avocados
Juice of 1 lime
2 tablespoons minced fresh parsley
Salt and freshly ground black pepper
3 to 4 corn tortillas

Heat the 1 tablespoon oil in a large pot over medium heat. Add the garlic and cook until fragrant, about 30 seconds. Stir in 1 cup of the salsa and the broth and simmer for 5 minutes. Remove from the heat and allow to cool slightly.

Halve and pit one of the avocados and place it in a blender or food processor. Add the soup mixture and process until smooth. Transfer back to the pot, add the lime juice and parsley, and season to taste with salt and pepper. Simmer over low heat while you toast the tortillas.

Lightly brush the tortillas with oil and cut them into thin strips, about ¼ inch wide by 2 inches long. Heat a skillet over medium heat. Add the tortilla strips and cook until golden brown on both sides, about 3 minutes.

Just before serving, halve, pit, and dice the remaining avocado and stir half of it into the soup. To serve, garnish the soup with the remaining diced avocado, remaining ½ cup salsa, and the tortilla strips.

quicker fix

. . . .

Garnish with corn chips (whole or crumbled) instead of the tortilla strips.

alphabet vegetable soup

serves 4

Alphabet soup is a nostalgic favorite and this one is ready in minutes—not quite as fast as opening a can of prepared soup, but way more flavorful—and is homemade. The speedy secrets include using one of the vegetable broth shortcuts on page 15 and easy-to-prepare vegetables. If you'd rather use fresh vegetables instead of frozen, be sure to slice them thin, so they cook faster. Fresh carrots, celery, and zucchini are good choices, as are green beans and corn kernels.

1 tablespoon extra-virgin olive oil
1 large clove garlic, minced
3 scallions, chopped
4 cups vegetable broth (page 15)
1 (16-ounce) package frozen mixed
   vegetables

1 (16-ounce) can chickpeas, drained and
   rinsed
1 (15-ounce) can petite diced tomatoes,
   drained
Salt and freshly ground black pepper
⅓ cup alphabet-shaped soup pasta
2 tablespoons chopped fresh parsley

Heat the oil in a large saucepan over medium heat. Add the garlic and scallions. Cook until softened, about 3 minutes.

Stir in the broth, turn the heat to high, and bring to a boil. Stir in the mixed vegetables, chickpeas, and tomatoes. Season to taste with salt and pepper. Cook for 5 minutes, then add the pasta.

Decrease the heat to medium and simmer until the vegetables and pasta are tender, about 10 minutes. Add the parsley and taste and adjust the seasonings. Serve hot.

variation

Chopped yellow onion may be used instead of the scallions and/or garlic. Cooked vegetables that you have on hand can be added to the soup during the last five minutes.

chipotle-kissed black bean soup

serves 4

The smoky rich flavor of the chipotle helps make this soup taste like it's been simmering all day.

1 tablespoon extra-virgin olive oil
1 cup sliced baby carrots
¾ cup chopped onions
2 cloves garlic, minced
½ teaspoon ground cumin
3 (16-ounce) cans black beans, drained and
  rinsed

1 (15-ounce) can diced tomatoes, drained
3 cups vegetable broth (page 15)
1 to 2 canned chipotle chiles in adobo
  sauce, minced
Salt and freshly ground black pepper
Minced fresh cilantro or parsley,
  for garnish

Heat the oil in a large pot over medium heat. Add the carrots, onions, and garlic. Cover and cook until softened, about 5 minutes. Stir in the cumin, black beans, and tomatoes.

Add the broth and the chipotle and season with salt and pepper to taste. Simmer until the vegetables are soft and the flavors have developed, about 15 minutes.

Use an immersion blender to puree some of the soup right in the pot. If you don't have an immersion blender, transfer 2 to 3 cups of the soup to a blender or food processor and puree until smooth. Stir back into the pot. Taste and adjust the seasonings. Serve hot, garnished with cilantro or parsley.

chickpea and tomato soup with ditalini

serves 4

A nearly infinite variety of variations on the classic bean and pasta soup can be found throughout Italy. No wonder it's so popular—it's hearty, filling, and delicious. This soup can also be made with leftover cooked pasta—just add during the last few minutes to heat up.

1 tablespoon extra-virgin olive oil
½ cup chopped onions
1 tablespoon minced garlic
1 (15-ounce) can crushed tomatoes
¼ teaspoon dried oregano
Red pepper flakes

2 bay leaves
1 (16-ounce) can chickpeas, drained and rinsed
4 cups vegetable broth (page 15)
Salt and freshly ground black pepper
½ cup ditalini or other small pasta shapes

Heat the oil in a large saucepan over medium heat. Add the onions and garlic. Cover and cook until softened, about 5 minutes. Stir in the tomatoes, oregano, red pepper flakes to taste, and bay leaves. Add the chickpeas and broth, and season to taste with salt and pepper. Simmer to blend the flavors, about 10 minutes. Add the ditalini and cook until tender, 6 to 8 minutes more. Remove the bay leaves before serving.

serving suggestion

When served with a salad and toasted garlic bread, this makes an easy and economical meal.

mushroom and white bean soup

serves 4

To brighten the flavor of the soup slightly, add a splash of sherry during the last 5 minutes of cooking time. Another nice change is to use different herbs, according to preference and what's available. One suggestion is to substitute fresh dill for both the dried savory and fresh parsley.

1 tablespoon extra-virgin olive oil
½ cup chopped onions
1 pound mushrooms, sliced
1 teaspoon dried savory
4 cups vegetable broth (page 15)

1 (16-ounce) can Great Northern beans or other white beans, drained and rinsed
Salt and freshly ground black pepper
2 tablespoons chopped fresh parsley

Heat the oil in a large pot over medium heat. Add the onions, cover, and cook until softened, about 5 minutes. Stir in the mushrooms, savory, and broth. Bring to a boil. Decrease the heat to low, add the beans, and season to taste with salt and pepper. Simmer to heat through and develop the flavor, about 10 minutes. Use an immersion blender to puree some of the soup right in the pot. If you don't have an immersion blender, transfer about 2 cups of the soup to a blender or food processor and puree until smooth. Stir back into the pot. Taste and adjust the seasonings and heat until hot, about 5 minutes. To serve, ladle into bowls and sprinkle with the parsley.

quicker fix

Buy presliced mushrooms.

minestrone in minutes

serves 4

The classic Italian vegetable soup typically includes a wide variety of vegetables. Using frozen vegetables reduces the prep time as well as the cooking time, but fresh vegetables may be used instead if you prefer. Cooked pasta, rice, or orzo added at the last minute would make a hearty addition. A spoonful of pesto can add volumes of flavor. Use this recipe as more of a guide than gospel.

1 tablespoon extra-virgin olive oil
½ cup chopped onions
1 large clove garlic, minced
1 (16-ounce) package frozen Italian
  vegetables
1 (15-ounce) can diced tomatoes, undrained
1 (16-ounce) can chickpeas, drained and
  rinsed

5 cups vegetable broth (page 15)
1 teaspoon dried basil
¼ teaspoon dried oregano
Salt and freshly ground black pepper
3 cups fresh baby spinach, firmly packed
2 tablespoons minced fresh parsley

Heat the oil in a large pot over medium heat. Add the onions and garlic. Cover and cook until softened, about 5 minutes. Stir in the frozen vegetables, tomatoes and their juice, chickpeas, and broth. Add the basil, oregano, and salt and pepper to taste. Bring to a boil, then decrease the heat to low and simmer for 20 minutes. A few minutes before serving time, stir in the spinach and parsley. Taste and adjust the seasonings.

cream of pumpkin soup topped with curried pecans

serves 4

Creamy and delicious with a delightful crunch of nuts, this sweet and spicy soup is a great way to begin an autumn meal.

1 tablespoon extra-virgin olive oil
¼ cup chopped onions
2 tablespoons curry powder
1 (15-ounce) can pumpkin puree
2 cups vegetable broth (page 15)

2 tablespoons pure maple syrup
Salt and freshly ground black pepper
¼ cup pecan pieces
1 (14-ounce) can light unsweetened
   coconut milk

Preheat the oven to 375°F. Heat the oil in a large pot over medium heat. Add the onions. Cover and cook until softened, about 5 minutes. Stir in 1 tablespoon of the curry powder and the pumpkin puree, then whisk in the broth until smooth. Add 1 tablespoon of the maple syrup and season to taste with salt and pepper. Simmer, stirring occasionally, for 10 minutes to allow the flavors to develop.

While the soup is simmering, make the curried pecans. In a small bowl, combine the pecan pieces with the remaining tablespoon of maple syrup and toss to coat. Sprinkle with the remaining 1 tablespoon curry powder, tossing to coat. Place the pecans in a small baking dish and bake until toasted, about 10 minutes. Set aside to cool.

Meanwhile, use an immersion blender to puree the soup right in the pot. Otherwise, transfer the soup to a blender or food processor and puree until smooth. Stir back into the pot. Return the soup to the stove top, turning the heat to low. Whisk in the coconut milk and taste and adjust the seasonings. Heat until hot; do not boil. Serve the soup garnished with the pecans.

corn chowder with limas

serves 4

This luxurious corn chowder includes lima beans as an homage to succotash. Because baby limas are smaller than the larger ones, they take less time to cook. To cut cooking time further, heat the vegetable broth in the microwave for 5 minutes while the onions and potato are cooking.

1 tablespoon extra-virgin olive oil
½ cup chopped onions
1 white potato, cut into ¼-inch dice
3 cups vegetable broth (page 15)
2 cups frozen baby lima beans

3 cups frozen corn kernels
1½ cups soy milk
Salt and freshly ground black pepper
1 tablespoon chopped pimientos

Heat the oil in a large pot over medium heat. Add the onions and potato, cover, and cook until softened, about 5 minutes. Add the broth and bring to a boil. Stir in the limas and corn and cook until tender, about 15 minutes. Decrease the heat to low, stir in the soy milk, and season to taste with salt and pepper. Use an immersion blender to puree some of the soup right in the pot. If you don't have an immersion blender, transfer about 2 cups of the soup to a blender or food processor and puree until smooth. Stir back into the pot. Reheat the soup if necessary. Ladle the soup into bowls and garnish with the pimientos.

red lentil soup

serves 4

Red lentils are the quickest-cooking variety of lentils, making them an ideal candidate for a quick soup. Curry powder adds an Indian flavor, making this soup reminiscent of dal, the savory lentil and bean dish of India.

1 tablespoon extra-virgin olive oil
1 bunch scallions, chopped
1 tablespoon curry powder
1 cup red lentils, picked over and rinsed
1 (15-ounce) can petite diced tomatoes,
   drained

4 cups vegetable broth (page 15)
Salt and freshly ground black pepper
1 zucchini, halved lengthwise
1 cup water, as needed

Heat the oil in a large saucepan over medium heat. Add the scallions and the curry powder and cook until fragrant, about 30 seconds. Stir in the lentils, tomatoes, and broth, and bring to a boil. Decrease the heat to low, season to taste with salt and pepper, and simmer for 10 minutes. While the lentils are simmering, thinly slice the zucchini and add it to the soup. Add up to 1 cup of water if the soup is too thick. Cook until the lentils are soft, about 10 minutes more.

variations

Instead of using zucchini, try small cauliflower florets, cut green beans, or chopped spinach or chard. You can also add leftover or precooked vegetables during the last few minutes; cook just long enough to heat them through.

barley and bean soup with rainbow chard

serves 4

Wholesome and hearty, this soup is especially good on a cold winter day, and because it's made with quick-cooking barley, it can be ready in minutes.

1 tablespoon extra-virgin olive oil
2 cloves garlic, minced
5 cups vegetable broth (page 15)
¾ cup quick-cooking pearl barley
Salt and freshly ground black pepper

1 bunch rainbow chard, leaves halved lengthwise, then cut crosswise into thin strips
1 (16-ounce) can cannellini beans, drained and rinsed

Heat the oil in a large saucepan over medium heat. Add the garlic and cook until fragrant, about 30 seconds. Add the broth and bring to a boil. Stir in the barley and salt and pepper to taste. Decrease the heat to low. Add the chard and beans and simmer until the barley is cooked, about 15 minutes.

note: Regular Swiss chard may be used if rainbow chard is unavailable.

phast phresh pho

serves 4

Pho, pronounced *fuh*, is a hearty Vietnamese soup traditionally made with beef. In this quick and tasty, albeit nontraditional, version, seitan, or wheat meat, replaces the beef. Look for seitan in the refrigerated section of natural food stores. If you can't find it, substitute one of the vegetarian "beef" strip products available under different brand names. Fresh rice noodles help with the speed of this recipe, but, as noted below, linguine makes a good substitute.

5 cups water
2 teaspoons fresh or bottled minced ginger
¼ cup hoisin sauce
1 teaspoon chili paste
1 bunch scallions, minced
4 ounces seitan, cut into strips
6 ounces fresh flat rice noodles (see Note)

2 tablespoons tamari
2 tablespoons freshly squeezed lime juice
2 tablespoons dark miso paste
1 teaspoon toasted sesame oil
¾ cup fresh bean sprouts
¼ cup chopped fresh cilantro

Bring the water to a boil in a large pot over high heat. Add the ginger, hoisin, chili paste, and half of the scallions. Decrease the heat to low and simmer for 15 minutes. Stir in the seitan, noodles, tamari, and lime juice.

Remove ½ cup of the hot liquid to a small bowl. Stir the miso paste into the liquid to blend well, then return to the soup. Stir in the sesame oil and bean sprouts; simmer for 3 minutes to blend the flavors.

To serve, ladle the soup into a large tureen or individual bowls and garnish with the cilantro and the remaining scallions. Serve hot.

note: Fresh rice noodles are available at Asian markets. They are cooked and ready to use in recipes. If unavailable, use dried rice noodles and prepare according to package directions. Otherwise, this recipe can also be made with linguine.

miso soup with soba and watercress

serves 4

Miso is made from aged soybeans combined with a grain or other ingredient into a salty paste. Flavors range from a light mellow white miso made with rice to boldly assertive brown miso made with barley. Soba noodles are made from buckwheat. Add diced baked tofu at the end for a heartier soup.

4 cups water
2 bunches watercress, chopped
¼ cup minced scallions

1 tablespoon tamari
4 ounces soba (buckwheat) noodles
3 tablespoons white miso paste

Bring the water to a boil in a large pot over high heat. Add the watercress, scallions, and tamari. Add the noodles, decrease the heat to medium, and simmer until the noodles are tender, about 5 minutes. Decrease the heat to low.

Place about ¼ cup of the hot soup mixture in a small bowl and add the miso paste, blending well. Stir the blended miso mixture back into the soup and simmer for 2 minutes, being careful not to boil. Serve hot.

hot and sour noodle soup

serves 4

Frozen stir-fry vegetables are the secret to the speed of preparing this flavorful Asian soup. If you have extra time, chop some fresh vegetables to replace the frozen ones. Celery, carrots, and bok choy are good choices. Snow peas make a good addition as well.

1 tablespoon canola oil
2 teaspoons minced garlic
2 teaspoons fresh or bottled minced ginger
1 (16-ounce) package frozen Asian vegetables for stir-fry, thawed
2 cups vegetable broth (page 15)
2 cups water

2 tablespoons tamari
2 tablespoons rice vinegar
½ teaspoon chili paste, or to taste
4 ounces thin Asian noodles or linguine pasta
2 tablespoons chopped scallions
1 tablespoon toasted sesame oil

Heat the canola oil in a large saucepan over medium heat. Add the garlic, ginger, and stir-fry vegetables and cook, stirring occasionally, for 2 minutes.

Stir in the broth, water, tamari, vinegar, and chili paste. Bring to a boil over high heat, add the noodles, then decrease the heat to medium and cook until the noodles and vegetables are tender, about 10 minutes.

Stir in the scallions and sesame oil. Taste and adjust the seasonings, adding more tamari if needed. Serve hot.

chilled cucumber avocado soup

serves 4

Cucumber and avocado team up for a refreshing chilled soup that is light yet rich-tasting and creamy. This recipe makes enough for four small bowls to serve as a lovely first course but can easily be doubled if you want more soup. I think the radish makes an interesting garnish, but the soup could also be garnished with some minced parsley, a small slice of avocado or cucumber, or some diced tomato.

2 ripe Hass avocados
2 English cucumbers, halved, seeded, and
   cut into chunks
1¼ cups soy milk
2 tablespoons chopped scallions

1 tablespoon freshly squeezed lime juice
¾ teaspoon salt, plus additional to taste
Freshly ground black pepper
1 red radish, sliced paper thin

Halve and pit the avocados. Scoop out the flesh with a spoon and place it in a food processor. Add the cucumbers and process until pureed. Add the soy milk, scallions, lime juice, salt, and pepper to taste and process until smooth. Taste and adjust the seasonings. Transfer the soup to a container and refrigerate until chilled. To serve, ladle the soup into bowls and garnish with the sliced radish.

fast and fresh gazpacho

serves 4 to 6

If you prefer your gazpacho more on the spicy side, begin with a spicy tomato-vegetable juice, such as Spicy Hot V8, or serve with the Tabasco bottle handy, so hot-food lovers can spice the soup to their own taste. (Note: Since this soup benefits from chilling and sitting, it's best to make it several hours ahead of when you need it.)

3 large ripe tomatoes, coarsely chopped
2 English cucumbers, halved, seeded, and chopped
1 bunch scallions, coarsely chopped
2 cloves garlic, minced
1 red or yellow bell pepper, chopped
2 tablespoons minced celery

1 tablespoon balsamic vinegar
½ teaspoon salt
¼ teaspoon Tabasco, or to taste
4 cups blended vegetable juice (such as V8)
¼ cup minced fresh parsley

In a food processor, combine two-thirds of the chopped tomatoes, one-half of the chopped cucumbers, the scallions, and the garlic and process until smooth.

Transfer the vegetable puree to a large bowl and add the bell pepper and the remaining cucumber and tomato. Stir in the celery, vinegar, salt, and Tabasco. Stir in the vegetable juice and 2 tablespoons of the parsley.

Cover the bowl and refrigerate for at least 2 hours to chill and blend the flavors. Taste and adjust the seasonings. Serve the soup chilled and garnished with the remaining 2 tablespoons parsley.

quicker fix

If you just don't have time to put this soup together ahead of time, try this trick: Freeze half of the vegetable juice in ice cube trays and chill the rest in the refrigerator. That way, when you assemble the soup later, the frozen juice will thaw into the rest of the soup ingredients, making for an icy cold soup when you need it.

quicker fix, too

To cut down on the amount of vegetables that need chopping, visit your supermarket salad bar and produce department for a selection of prechopped veggies.

chapter 4

salads that make the meal

With the presence of convenient salad bars and bagged greens in virtually every supermarket, making salads has never been easier. For those times when you want more than "just a salad"— that is also easy, economical, and satisfying, and that has your personal touch—it's good to have some great homemade salad recipes to rely on.

This chapter focuses primarily on hearty main-dish salads that can literally make the meal. Using a variety of leafy greens, crunchy vegetables, nuts, and fruits combined with pasta, grains, beans, and flavorful dressings, these recipes will add more variety and texture to your salads and provide tempting and creative main-dish ideas for lunch and dinner.

Recipes such as Black Bean and Rice Salad with Roasted Red Peppers and Corn; Quinoa Salad with Roasted Asparagus, White Beans, and Red Peppers; and Thai Noodle Salad with Peanut Sauce are hearty enough to be served as a meal. Lighter, leafier salads such as Mixed Baby Greens with Pears, Pecans, and Polenta Strips and Sesame-Spinach Salad with Mango are elegant ways to begin a special dinner.

mediterranean orzo salad

serves 4

This salad features the diminutive rice-shaped pasta called orzo enhanced by lusty Kalamata olives and crunchy toasted pine nuts.

1½ cups orzo
1 large clove garlic
2 tablespoons white wine vinegar
1 teaspoon Dijon mustard
½ teaspoon dried marjoram
¼ cup extra-virgin olive oil
½ teaspoon salt
Freshly ground black pepper
1 (16-ounce) can chickpeas, drained
   and rinsed

1 (6-ounce) jar marinated artichoke
   hearts, drained
½ cup oil-packed sun-dried tomatoes,
   cut into strips
½ cup pitted Kalamata olives
½ cup chopped fresh flat-leaf parsley
¼ cup minced scallions
Salad greens, for serving
¼ cup toasted pine nuts (page 21)

Cook the orzo in a pot of salted boiling water until tender, about 5 minutes. Drain and rinse under cold water.

While the orzo is cooking, mince the garlic in a food processor. Add the vinegar, mustard, marjoram, olive oil, salt, and pepper to taste. Process until well blended. Set the dressing aside.

In a large bowl, combine the cooked orzo, the chickpeas, artichoke hearts, sun-dried tomatoes, olives, parsley, and scallions. Pour the dressing over the salad, and toss gently to combine.

To serve, line a shallow bowl or individual plates with salad greens. Spoon the orzo salad onto the greens, and serve topped with the pine nuts.

southwestern pasta salad with avocado-serrano dressing

serves 4

Texture and flavor contrasts abound in this Southwestern-inspired salad. The buttery avocado helps to smooth the heat of the serrano chile in the dressing.

12 ounces penne pasta
1 serrano chile, seeded
1 large clove garlic
2 ripe Hass avocados
3 tablespoons freshly squeezed lime juice
½ teaspoon chili powder
¼ cup extra-virgin olive oil
Salt

1 (16-ounce) can pinto beans, drained and rinsed
1 small jicama, shredded
1 small red onion, chopped
1 cup grape or cherry tomatoes, halved
¼ cup chopped fresh parsley or cilantro
Salad greens, for serving

Put the pasta water on to boil. Cook the penne in the salted boiling water, stirring occasionally, until it is al dente, about 10 minutes.

While the pasta is cooking, make the dressing: Mince the chile and garlic in a food processor. Halve and pit one of the avocados, scoop out the flesh with a spoon, and add it to the food processor. Add the lime juice and chili powder and process until smooth. Add the olive oil, and salt to taste; process until smooth.

When the pasta is cooked, drain and rinse it under cold water, then place it in a large bowl. Add the beans, jicama, onion, tomatoes, and parsley. Peel, halve, pit, and dice the remaining avocado and add it to the pasta salad. Pour on the dressing and toss gently to combine. Serve on salad greens.

black bean and rice salad with roasted red peppers and corn

serves 4

This colorful and delicious salad is one you'll make again and again. It is especially quick to assemble if you begin with rice that has been cooked ahead.

1 cup raw quick-cooking brown rice,
   or 3 cups cooked
1 (16-ounce) can black beans, drained and
   rinsed
1 (16-ounce) can corn kernels, drained
1 (6-ounce) jar roasted red bell peppers,
   drained and chopped

2 scallions, minced
2 tablespoons freshly squeezed lime juice
¼ teaspoon chili powder
½ teaspoon salt
¼ cup extra-virgin olive oil
2 tablespoons minced fresh parsley
   or cilantro

If beginning with raw rice, cook it according to package directions. While the rice is cooking, combine the beans, corn, roasted red peppers, and scallions in a large bowl and set aside. When the rice is cooked, set it aside to cool while you make the dressing. When the rice is somewhat cooled, add it to the other salad ingredients in the large bowl. (If beginning with rice that has been cooked ahead, add it to the other salad ingredients now.)

In a small bowl, combine the lime juice, chili powder, and salt. Whisk in the oil. Pour the dressing onto the rice salad and toss lightly to coat. Taste and adjust the seasonings. Sprinkle with parsley and serve.

mixed baby greens with pears, pecans, and polenta strips

serves 4

Polenta strips make an unusual alternative to croutons in this delicious salad that combines the mellow sweetness of pears with the crunch of toasted pecans. Prepared polenta is available in the produce section of many supermarkets. It is sold in a log-shaped package. A shelf-stable cooked polenta is also available and can be found in the dried pasta section of many supermarkets.

1 (16-ounce) package precooked polenta
¼ cup extra-virgin olive oil, plus additional for brushing the polenta
Salt and freshly ground black pepper
4 cups fresh mixed baby greens
¼ cup chopped red onion

¼ cup minced celery
2 ripe pears
3 tablespoons freshly squeezed lemon juice
½ teaspoon light brown sugar
½ cup toasted pecans (page 21)

Preheat the oven to 400°F. Cut the polenta into ¼-inch-thick slices, then cut the slices into ¼-inch-thick strips. Place on a nonstick baking sheet, brush lightly with olive oil, sprinkle with salt and pepper, and bake, turning once, until slightly crisp, about 15 minutes total. Set aside to cool.

While the polenta is baking, make the salad. Place the greens in a large bowl. Add the red onion and celery. Peel, core, and dice or thinly slice the pears and place in a separate bowl. Add 1 tablespoon of the lemon juice and toss to combine. Add about three-quarters of the pears to the salad, reserving about one quarter of the diced pears.

Puree the reserved diced pears in a food processor. Add the remaining 2 tablespoons lemon juice, the brown sugar, and salt and pepper to taste. With the machine running, add the ¼ cup olive oil until blended. Pour the dressing over the salad and toss gently to combine. Sprinkle the salad with the pecans and top with the polenta strips.

shredded fennel, radicchio, and penne salad with bits of walnut and orange

serves 4

The licorice flavor of the fennel and the slight bitterness of radicchio play nicely against the sweet-tart dressing flavored with orange.

1 pound penne pasta
2 tablespoons freshly squeezed orange juice
2 tablespoons balsamic vinegar
3 tablespoons extra-virgin olive oil or walnut oil
1 teaspoon light brown sugar
1 teaspoon Dijon mustard

Salt and freshly ground black pepper
1 fennel bulb, shredded
1 head radicchio, quartered and cut into ¼-inch strips
½ cup chopped red onions (optional)
2 oranges, chopped
1 tablespoon chopped fresh parsley
¼ cup toasted walnuts pieces (page 21)

Add the penne to salted boiling water. Cook, stirring occasionally, until it is al dente, about 10 minutes. Drain and run under cold water to cool slightly.

While the pasta is cooking, make the vinaigrette. In a small bowl, combine the orange juice, vinegar, olive oil, brown sugar, mustard, and salt and pepper to taste. Whisk to combine well. Set aside.

In a large bowl, combine the fennel, radicchio, onions, and orange pieces. Add the cooked pasta and the vinaigrette. Toss gently to combine. Garnish with the walnuts and parsley.

tabbouleh with dried fruit and walnuts

serves 4

Sweet bits of dried fruit and crunchy nuts add a delightful twist to this Middle Eastern salad that is traditionally made with tomatoes and parsley. Use an individual dried fruit such as apricot or cranberry or a combination of your favorites. Serve on lettuce leaves.

1 cup bulgur
1 cup chopped dried fruit
1 cup walnut pieces
1 bunch scallions, chopped

½ cup chopped fresh mint
¼ cup walnut oil or extra-virgin olive oil
3 tablespoons freshly squeezed lemon juice
Salt and freshly ground black pepper

Add the bulgur to 2 cups of salted boiling water. Decrease the heat to low, cover, and simmer for 15 minutes, or until the water is absorbed. Drain any remaining water and blot the bulgur to remove the excess moisture.

Place the bulgur in a bowl and add the dried fruit. Toss to combine. Add the walnuts, scallions, and mint.

Pour on the walnut oil, lemon juice, and salt and pepper to taste. Toss well to combine.

quinoa salad with roasted asparagus, white beans, and red peppers

serves 4

If you've never tried quinoa, this is the salad to make if you want a tasty treat. Nutty, flavorful, and loaded with nutrients, quinoa is a delicious and underappreciated grain that shines when enhanced with this light lemony dressing, complemented by roasted asparagus.

1 cup quinoa, thoroughly rinsed
2 cups water
Salt
1 bunch thin asparagus, cut into
   2-inch pieces
¼ cup extra-virgin olive oil
Freshly ground black pepper
Juice of 1 lemon

1 (16-ounce) can white beans, drained
   and rinsed
1 (6-ounce) jar roasted red bell peppers,
   drained and cut into ¼ by 2-inch strips
½ cup thinly sliced celery
2 tablespoons minced scallions
Salad greens, for serving
2 tablespoons chopped fresh parsley
   or basil

Preheat the oven to 425°F. Combine the quinoa with the water in a saucepan and bring to a boil. Salt the water, reduce the heat to low, and simmer for 15 minutes, until all the liquid is absorbed. Drain well and place in a bowl. Set aside to cool.

Arrange the asparagus on a lightly oiled baking pan and drizzle with 1 tablespoon of the olive oil. Season to taste with salt and pepper. Roast until tender, about 8 minutes.

In a large bowl, combine the remaining 3 tablespoons olive oil, the lemon juice, and salt and pepper. Add the white beans, roasted red peppers, celery, and scallions, along with the roasted asparagus and cooked quinoa. Toss gently to combine. Serve on salad greens, garnished with the parsley.

thai noodle salad with peanut sauce

serves 4

This flavorful salad goes together quickly. Sure, you could use bottled peanut sauce in a pinch, but it's easy to make your own with handy pantry ingredients. Don't be afraid to vary the vegetables according to what's on hand and your own preference. For example, you might omit the carrot and tomatoes in favor of chopped red bell pepper and steamed broccoli florets.

8 ounces dried flat rice noodles or linguine
1 tablespoon toasted sesame oil
⅓ cup peanut butter
2 tablespoons freshly squeezed lime juice
1 tablespoon tamari
1 teaspoon light brown sugar

¼ teaspoon cayenne
1 large carrot, shredded
1 cup grape tomatoes, halved
1 cup frozen baby peas, thawed
¼ cup minced scallions

Cook the noodles in a large pot of boiling water according to package directions. Drain and rinse the noodles under cold water and transfer to a large bowl. Toss with the sesame oil to coat.

While the noodles are cooking, combine the peanut butter, lime juice, tamari, brown sugar, and cayenne in a large bowl, whisking to blend well. Add a small amount of water if necessary to make a smooth sauce. Set aside.

To the dressing in the bowl, add the carrot, tomatoes, peas, scallions, and the cooked noodles. Toss gently to combine. Serve at room temperature.

note: Ready-to-use fresh rice noodles may be used instead of dried.

quicker fix

Use bottled peanut sauce.

japanese soba salad

serves 4

Japanese soba noodles are hearty yet delicate noodles made from buckwheat. They are available in Asian markets and natural food stores.

1 (10-ounce) package soba (buckwheat) noodles
¼ cup toasted sesame oil
1 red bell pepper, cut into julienne strips
4 napa cabbage leaves, finely sliced
3 scallions, minced

2 tablespoons rice vinegar
1 teaspoon fresh or bottled minced ginger
¼ teaspoon sugar
Salt and freshly ground black pepper

Cook the noodles in a large pot of boiling water until just tender, about 5 minutes, stirring occasionally. Drain and rinse the noodles under cold water, then place them in a large bowl with 1 teaspoon of the sesame oil. Add the bell pepper, napa cabbage, and scallions, and set aside.

In a small bowl, combine the vinegar, ginger, sugar, and salt and pepper to taste. Whisk in the remaining oil until blended. Pour the dressing over the salad and toss to combine.

cellophane noodle salad

serves 4

Also known as bean thread noodles or glass noodles, cellophane noodles are made from mung bean flour and are used throughout Asia in soups, stir-fries, and salads. For a striking color accent, add some grated carrot to the salad. For more substance, add some baked tofu, cut into a small dice. Look for finely shredded "angel hair" cabbage if you can find it—it creates a more delicate salad.

4 ounces cellophane noodles
1 (8-ounce) package shredded cabbage (for coleslaw)
1 cup bean sprouts
1 English cucumber, halved, seeded, and thinly sliced
3 scallions, chopped
3 tablespoons chopped fresh cilantro
3 tablespoons rice vinegar

2 tablespoons freshly squeezed lime juice
1 tablespoon tamari
2 teaspoons light brown sugar
1 teaspoon minced garlic
3 tablespoons toasted sesame oil
½ teaspoon chili paste
2 tablespoons water
½ cup roasted peanuts, crushed or chopped

Bring a saucepan of water to a boil over high heat. Remove from the heat and add the noodles. Soak the noodles in the hot water until they are soft, about 5 minutes. Drain well and rinse under cold water. Cut the noodles into quarters to make them easier to manage and arrange on a platter.

In a large bowl, combine the shredded cabbage, bean sprouts, cucumber, scallions, and cilantro. Set aside.

In a small bowl, combine the vinegar, lime juice, tamari, brown sugar, garlic, sesame oil, chili paste, and water. Mix until blended. Pour the dressing over the vegetables and toss to combine well.

To serve, spoon the salad over the noodles and sprinkle with the peanuts.

quicker fix

. . . .

Use a bottled Asian salad dressing.

tahini green bean salad
with baked tofu

serves 4

Baked marinated lemon-pepper tofu is available in natural food stores. If unavailable, you can make your own or omit the tofu entirely for a lovely and elegant green bean salad. Gomasio is a blend of toasted sesame seeds and sea salt and is available in natural food stores.

12 ounces green beans, trimmed
¼ cup tahini (sesame paste)
1 clove garlic, minced
2 tablespoons toasted sesame oil
2 tablespoons mirin
2 tablespoons tamari
Juice of 1 lemon
3 scallions, minced

2 tablespoons chopped fresh parsley
Salad greens, for serving
8 ounces baked lemon-pepper tofu, cut into ¼-inch strips
1 cup grape or cherry tomatoes, halved
Toasted sesame seeds (page 21) or gomasio, for garnish

Steam the green beans until just tender, about 8 minutes. Run under cold water to preserve the color and stop the cooking process. Set aside.

In a bowl, combine the tahini, garlic, sesame oil, mirin, tamari, and lemon juice. Whisk to blend. In a large bowl, combine the cooked green beans, the scallions, and parsley with enough of the tahini sauce to coat the vegetables. Toss gently to coat the beans.

On a round platter lined with salad greens, arrange the green beans and tofu strips in a circular pattern. Mound the tomatoes in the center of the circle created by the beans and tofu. Drizzle the remaining sauce over all and sprinkle with sesame seeds.

chutney rice salad with pineapple and peanuts

serves 4

This fruity, flavorful rice salad is great for a lunch or casual supper. It's also a good addition to a party buffet. Next time you cook up some rice, make extra so you can put this salad together even faster.

1¼ cups quick-cooking brown rice
½ cup mango chutney
1 (8-ounce) can pineapple chunks, drained with juice reserved
Juice of 1 lime
2 teaspoons curry powder
Salt and freshly ground black pepper
1 small red bell pepper, cut into thin matchsticks
2 tablespoons minced scallions
Salad greens, for serving
¾ cup peanuts

Cook the rice according to package directions, about 10 minutes. Transfer the cooked rice to a large bowl and refrigerate to allow the rice to cool while you make the dressing.

In a blender or food processor, combine the chutney, reserved pineapple juice, lime juice, curry powder, and salt and pepper to taste, and process until well blended. Pour the dressing over the rice. Add the bell pepper, pineapple chunks, and scallions, and toss gently to combine. Serve on salad greens sprinkled with the peanuts.

sesame-spinach salad with mango

serves 4

The vibrant colors of spinach and mango combine in this dazzling sesame-dressed salad that is as beautiful as it is delicious.

1 tablespoon tahini (sesame paste)
2 tablespoons canola oil
1 tablespoon toasted sesame oil
1 tablespoon freshly squeezed lemon juice
1 tablespoon tamari
Salt and freshly ground black pepper

1 (10-ounce) package fresh spinach
1 ripe mango, halved, pitted, and cut into
   ½-inch dice
1 tablespoon toasted sesame seeds
   (see page 21)

Place the tahini in a bowl. Whisk in the canola oil and sesame oil until smooth. Whisk in the lemon juice and tamari. Season to taste with salt and pepper. Set aside.

Tear the spinach into bite-sized pieces and place in a salad bowl. Add the mango and the dressing. Toss to combine. Sprinkle with the toasted sesame seeds.

variations

Add chopped red bell pepper or diced avocado to the salad.

waldorf-inspired coleslaw

serves 4 to 6

Crisp apples and crunchy walnuts are just two of the taste treats in this luscious slaw inspired by the classic Waldorf salad.

1 cup raw cashews
½ cup apple juice
2 tablespoons freshly squeezed lemon juice
½ teaspoon sugar
¼ teaspoon salt
2 apples, halved and cored

1 (8-ounce) package shredded cabbage (for coleslaw)
½ cup walnut pieces
¼ cup golden raisins or sweetened dried cranberries
2 scallions, finely minced

In a blender or food processor, grind the cashews to a fine powder. Add the apple juice and process until smooth. Add the lemon juice, sugar, and salt, and process until well blended. Transfer the dressing to a large bowl.

Thinly slice the apples and add to the dressing. Toss gently to coat the apples with the dressing. Add the shredded cabbage to the bowl, along with the walnuts, raisins, and scallions. Stir to combine well. Taste and adjust the seasonings.

warm potato salad with cherry tomatoes and fresh basil

serves 4

Look for the smallest red potatoes you can find, sometimes called B reds or creamer potatoes. If larger potatoes are used, you will need to cut them into smaller pieces so that they will cook quickly.

1½ pounds very small red potatoes, halved
   or quartered
½ cup extra-virgin olive oil
3 tablespoons white wine vinegar

Pinch of sugar
Salt and freshly ground black pepper
1½ cups cherry or grape tomatoes, halved
½ cup firmly packed fresh basil leaves

Cook the potatoes in a saucepan of salted boiling water until just tender, 12 to 15 minutes. While the potatoes are cooking, make the dressing.

In a bowl, combine the oil, vinegar, sugar, and salt and pepper to taste. When the potatoes are cooked, drain them well and toss gently with the dressing. Add the tomatoes and basil, tossing gently to combine. Taste and adjust the seasonings, adding more salt and pepper if needed. Serve warm or at room temperature.

variations

Minced garlic or scallions may be added to the salad, if desired.

meze in minutes

serves 4

Imagine serving an impressive meze platter on the table in just minutes. The secret is to use prepared tabbouleh, hummus, and dolmas from the deli case. The more time you have, the more "homemade" elements you can include, such as your own tabbouleh and hummus, that you can make ahead.

1 head romaine lettuce, shredded
1½ cups hummus, store-bought or
   homemade (page 33)
2 cups tabbouleh, store-bought or
   homemade (page 67)
12 ounces dolmas, canned or from the deli

½ cup imported black olives
1 ripe tomato, cut into wedges
1 lemon, cut into wedges
2 (7-inch) pita bread rounds, cut into
   eighths

Line a large platter with the shredded romaine. Place the hummus in a bowl and set in the center of the platter.

Divide the tabbouleh in half and arrange each half in a mound on opposite sides of the bowl of hummus.

Divide the dolmas in half and stack each half in a pile on the remaining opposite sides of the hummus.

Arrange the olives and tomato and lemon wedges decoratively on the platter, filling in gaps between the dolmas and tabbouleh.

Warm the pita bread and serve alongside the meze platter, or if your platter is large enough, arrange the pita triangles on the platter as well, dividing them into two piles between the tabbouleh and dolmas.

sandwiches and wraps

Sandwiches are quick and convenient solutions to getting food on the table. And since they usually travel well, they can be ideal candidates to pack in a lunch box. Sometimes, however, we may find ourselves in a sandwich rut, perhaps slathering bread with peanut butter and jelly, day after day.

To remedy the same old sandwich routine, this chapter is filled with tantalizing and creative sandwich recipes that reach beyond the PB&J but are every bit as delicious.

From wraps to Reubens, these full-flavored sandwiches are fit for a filling lunch or a casual supper. With choices ranging from the hearty Potato "Dosadillas" and Oh-So-Sloppy Joes, to the light and flavorful Avocado Salad Wraps and Grilled Garden Sandwiches, there's something to please every mood and palate, including a sophisticated twist on the peanut butter sandwich: Peanut Butter and Tomato Quesadillas.

potato "dosadillas"

serves 2 to 4

Southern India meets Mexico in this dosa-quesadilla hybrid I created one day when I was craving the fabulous dosas made at my local Indian restaurant. Using what I had on hand, I came amazingly close to the flavor of authentic dosas with a minimum of effort. Although this recipe is in the sandwich chapter, it makes a satisfying dinner entrée as well. If you have some leftover cooked veggies that you'd like to use instead of the peas, chop them and mix them in with the potatoes. Use hot or mild curry paste or powder, according to taste.

1 tablespoon extra-virgin olive oil
2 tablespoons minced scallions or onion
2 cups mashed potatoes (see Note)
½ cup frozen baby peas, thawed

1½ teaspoons curry paste or powder, plus additional to taste
4 large whole wheat tortillas

Heat the oil in a small skillet. Add the scallions and cook until softened. Add the potatoes, peas, and curry paste and cook until well mixed and hot. If you like spicy food, add a little more curry to taste.

Divide the mixture evenly over half of each of the tortillas. Fold the tortillas over and place them, two at a time, in a large nonstick skillet or griddle over medium heat. Cook, turning once, until lightly browned on both sides. Keep them warm while you cook the remaining dosadillas. Serve them whole to be cut with a knife and fork, or cut them into wedges to eat out of hand.

note: The mashed potatoes can come from a variety of sources: You can plan ahead and make extra baked or mashed potatoes for dinner the night before, putting the extra aside for this recipe. If there was ever a reason to make extra potatoes, this is it.

If you don't have cooked potatoes on hand, you can quickly microwave some and then simply mash them with a potato masher, adding salt and pepper and a little margarine. In a pinch, instant mashed potatoes can also be used (the prominent curry flavor of the filling masks the "instant potato" taste).

serving suggestion
. . . .

Serve with mint or tamarind chutney, raita, or a vegetable sambar.

lemon-braised
tofu-hummus wraps

serves 4

Soft tortillas, crisp romaine, and creamy tofu are the perfect complement for the flavorful hummus. The Green Onion Hummus with Lime on page 33 is especially good in this sandwich, but regular hummus would be delicious as well.

2 tablespoons extra-virgin olive oil
1 pound extra-firm tofu, cut into ¼-inch
    strips
¼ teaspoon lemon pepper seasoning
Salt

Juice of 2 lemons
4 large flour tortillas
¼ cup Green Onion Hummus with Lime
    (page 33) or regular hummus
2 cups chopped romaine lettuce

Heat the oil in a large skillet over medium-high heat. Add the tofu and the lemon pepper seasoning and season with salt. Cook, stirring frequently, until golden brown, about 5 minutes each side. Drizzle the lemon juice onto the tofu, stirring to coat. Transfer to a plate to cool.

To fill the wraps, spread the hummus on the tortillas, top with the tofu and romaine, and roll up. Cut in half to serve.

quicker fix

To make these sandwiches at the speed of light, buy a container of prepared hummus and a package of baked lemon-pepper tofu.

mediterranean muffuletta sandwich

serves 4

Thinly sliced pan-seared portobello mushrooms replace the traditional meat in this delicious interpretation of the classic New Orleans sandwich.

¼ cup extra-virgin olive oil, plus additional
   for drizzling
3 large portobello mushroom caps, cut into
   ¼-inch slices
Salt and freshly ground black pepper
2 tablespoons balsamic vinegar
1 cup chopped pimiento-stuffed green
   olives

½ cup chopped bottled roasted red bell
   peppers
½ cup chopped bottled peperoncini
   peppers
½ cup green or black olive tapenade,
   bottled or homemade (page 18)
¼ cup chopped oil-packed sun-dried
   tomatoes
1 round loaf Italian bread

Heat 2 tablespoons of the oil in a large skillet over medium-high heat. Add the mushroom slices and sear on both sides. Season to taste with salt and pepper and drizzle with the balsamic vinegar. Cook until the mushrooms are tender, about 5 minutes. Transfer to a plate and allow to cool.

In a medium bowl, combine the olives, roasted red peppers, peperoncini, tapenade, sun-dried tomatoes, and the remaining tablespoon oil. Season to taste with salt and pepper and set aside.

Carefully cut the loaf of bread in half horizontally, using a serrated bread knife. Pinch out some of the inside of the loaf to make room for the filling.

Drizzle a small amount of olive oil on the cut side of both halves of the bread. Spread half of the olive mixture on the bottom half of the bread. Layer the mushrooms on top, then spread the remaining olive mixture evenly on top of the mushrooms. Replace the top half of the bread. To serve, cut the loaf into quarters.

quicker fix

. . . .

Replace the mushrooms with sliced vegetarian ham and cheese.

oyster mushroom po'boys

serves 2

Oyster mushrooms stand in for the traditional oysters in this popular Louisiana sandwich. If panko bread crumbs are unavailable, regular dried bread crumbs may be used.

8 ounces oyster mushrooms, trimmed and cut into bite-sized pieces
3 tablespoons extra-virgin olive oil
Salt and freshly ground black pepper
¾ cup panko (Japanese) bread crumbs
½ teaspoon Old Bay seasoning

2 (6-inch) sub rolls
2 tablespoons soy mayonnaise
3 romaine lettuce leaves, cut crosswise into ¼-inch strips
1 large ripe tomato, sliced
Tabasco

In a bowl, toss the mushrooms with 1 tablespoon of the oil and season with salt and pepper to taste. Add the bread crumbs and Old Bay seasoning and toss gently to coat the mushrooms. Set aside.

Heat the remaining 2 tablespoons oil in a large skillet over medium heat. Add the mushrooms and cook until golden brown all over. Remove from the heat and set aside.

Split the rolls in half lengthwise and spread the cut sides with the mayonnaise. Line the bottom half of each roll with lettuce. Arrange the tomato slices on top, followed by the oyster mushrooms. Sprinkle with Tabasco to taste, and replace the top half of the rolls. Serve with the bottle of Tabasco on the table.

peanut butter and tomato quesadillas

serves 2

If you think grape jelly is the only suitable partner for peanut butter, you're in for a pleasant surprise with this delicious quesadilla. Best to make this only when fresh ripe tomatoes are at their peak. Crisply fried tempeh bacon makes a good addition. A sprinkle of red pepper flakes would add a spicy note. This recipe is easily doubled.

2 soft flour tortillas
⅓ cup creamy peanut butter

6 very thin slices large ripe tomato
Salt and freshly ground black pepper

Spread the tortillas with the peanut butter and arrange 3 slices of tomato on top of the peanut butter on one-half of each tortilla. Season with salt and pepper to taste.

Fold the tortillas in half to enclose the tomatoes and peanut butter. Place both quesadillas in a large nonstick skillet and cook, turning once, until lightly browned on both sides.

To serve, transfer the quesadillas to a cutting board and cut them into wedges.

oh-so-sloppy joes

serves 4

Frozen veggie burger crumbles make great and superquick sloppy joes. If unavailable, chop up a package of thawed frozen veggie burgers.

1 tablespoon extra-virgin olive oil
¼ cup chopped onion
1 (12-ounce) package frozen vegetarian
   burger crumbles
1 (4-ounce) can diced mild green chiles,
   drained

¾ cup tomato ketchup
3 tablespoons yellow mustard
2 tablespoons sweet pickle relish
Salt and freshly ground black pepper
4 sandwich buns

Heat the oil in a large skillet over medium heat. Add the onion, cover, and cook until softened, about 5 minutes. Add the burger crumbles and chiles. Stir in the ketchup, mustard, and pickle relish. Season to taste with salt and pepper. Simmer, stirring occasionally, until hot, about 10 minutes.

To serve, spoon the sloppy joe mixture into the buns and accompany with plenty of napkins.

california club sandwiches

serves 2

Buttery avocado and tempeh bacon put a new spin on the old-fashioned club sandwich. A juicy ripe tomato and good bread make it even better.

1 tablespoon extra-virgin olive oil
8 slices tempeh bacon
4 slices whole grain bread
2 tablespoons soy mayonnaise
2 romaine lettuce leaves

1 large ripe tomato, thinly sliced
1 ripe Hass avocado, halved, pitted, and thinly sliced
Salt and freshly ground black pepper

Heat the oil in a large skillet over medium heat. Add the tempeh bacon and cook, turning once, until browned on both sides, about 5 minutes total. Remove from the skillet and drain on paper towels.

Lightly toast the bread and spread with the soy mayonnaise. Place 2 slices of the prepared toast on a cutting board. Layer each slice with lettuce, tomato, avocado, and the tempeh bacon. Season to taste with salt and pepper. Top each with the remaining toast. Use a serrated bread knife to cut each sandwich in half diagonally and serve at once.

avocado salad wraps

serves 2

These wraps are like having your salad in a sandwich—fun to eat and pretty, too, especially if you use colorful spinach or tomato tortillas. Regular flour tortillas may be used if the vegetable tortillas are unavailable.

2 ripe Hass avocados, halved and pitted
1 tablespoon freshly squeezed lemon or
   lime juice
Salt and freshly ground black pepper
2 large spinach or tomato flour tortillas

1 English cucumber, seeded and thinly
   sliced
1 ripe tomato, thinly sliced
1 carrot, grated

Mash the avocado in a bowl with the lemon juice and salt and pepper to taste. Place the tortillas on a flat work surface and spread the avocado mixture evenly over both tortillas.

Arrange the cucumber, tomato, and carrot on top of the avocado mixture. Season with salt and pepper to taste. Roll up the filled tortillas and cut each in half with a serrated knife.

variations
· ·

Add more vegetables to the filling ingredients, such as alfalfa sprouts or red or yellow bell pepper strips.

curried tofu "egg salad" pitas

serves 4

Tofu performs remarkably well standing in for eggs in these protein-rich, cholesterol-free sandwiches. I especially like it stuffed in pitas, but you can serve it on rolls, in wraps, or on any bread you prefer.

1 pound extra-firm tofu, drained and
   crumbled
½ cup soy mayonnaise
1½ teaspoons Dijon mustard
1½ teaspoons curry powder
Salt and freshly ground black pepper

½ cup shredded carrots
2 scallions, finely minced
4 (7-inch) pita bread rounds, halved
   crosswise
1 cup shredded lettuce

Place the tofu in a large bowl. Add the mayonnaise, mustard, curry powder, and salt and pepper to taste. Mix well, then stir in the carrots and scallions until well combined.

To assemble the sandwiches, spoon the tofu mixture into each pita half. Tuck some of the lettuce into each sandwich for color and crunch.

variations

Add chopped red bell pepper or celery, or some sweet pickle relish.

rockin' reubens

serves 4

Tempeh is usually the designated meat replacement in a veggie Reuben sandwich. Here the tempeh gets some extra flavor from braising with the sauerkraut.

1 (8-ounce) package tempeh, cut in
⅛-inch-thick slices
1 cup sauerkraut
¼ cup soy mayonnaise
2 tablespoons tomato ketchup

2 tablespoons sweet pickle relish
Salt and freshly ground black pepper
3 tablespoons nonhydrogenated margarine
8 slices pumpernickel bread
4 slices soy cheese (optional)

Poach the tempeh in a saucepan of simmering water for 8 minutes. Drain the water from the saucepan and add the sauerkraut. Cover and cook over low heat for 5 minutes. Remove the tempeh and sauerkraut from the saucepan and set aside to cool.

Meanwhile, in a small bowl, combine the soy mayonnaise, ketchup, and pickle relish. Season with salt and pepper to taste. Blend well and set aside.

Spread the margarine onto one side of each slice of bread. Spread the mayonnaise mixture on the remaining side of each slice of bread and place 2 of the bread slices, margarine side down, in a large skillet.

Arrange one-quarter of the tempeh and sauerkraut on the bread in the skillet and top each with a slice of cheese and another slice of prepared the bread, margarine side up.

Cook the sandwiches in the skillet, turning once, until browned on both sides, about 3 minutes per side. Repeat with the remaining ingredients to make 2 more sandwiches.

grilled garden sandwiches

serves 4

Here are some quick ones for the grill. Use a mesh or perforated basket to prevent the vegetables from falling through the grill. If you don't have a grill, you can broil the vegetables or sear them in a skillet. Serve on toasted hard rolls.

1 large red onion, sliced
1 large yellow bell pepper, sliced
4 large portobello mushroom caps, gills scraped out
3 tablespoons extra-virgin olive oil

Salt and freshly ground black pepper
1 or 2 large ripe tomatoes, sliced
3 tablespoons basil pesto, bottled or homemade (page 17)
4 kaiser rolls or other hearty sandwich rolls

Preheat the grill. Brush the onion, bell pepper, and mushrooms with some of the olive oil and season them with salt and pepper. Grill the vegetables, turning once, until tender on the inside and slightly charred on the outside. Brush the tomato slices with oil and grill just long enough to char slightly on the outside.

Spread about 2 teaspoons of pesto onto each roll and fill with the grilled vegetables. Serve hot.

variations

Sliced zucchini may be used instead of or in addition to the bell pepper or mushrooms.

artichoke-hummus wraps
with spinach tortillas

serves 4

Hummus wraps are an ideal fast-food lunch idea, made even faster when you have some rich, creamy hummus on hand. Make your own or choose from the wide variety of hummus flavors available in supermarkets. If spinach tortillas are unavailable, regular flour tortillas may be used.

1 cup hummus, store-bought or homemade
   (page 33)
4 large spinach flour tortillas
1 (12-ounce) jar marinated artichoke hearts,
   drained and chopped

2 cups chopped romaine lettuce
1 carrot, grated
Salt and freshly ground black pepper

Spread about ¼ cup of the hummus on each of the tortillas. Top with the chopped artichokes, followed by the lettuce and carrot. Season to taste with salt and pepper. Tightly roll up the tortillas. To serve, cut in half and arrange on plates.

skillet suppers— flashes in the pan

From the haute cuisine of French sautés to the lightning-quick Asian stir-fries, a hot pan and quick-cooking ingredients are at the heart of many recipes throughout the world.

In this chapter, you will discover delicious "flash in the pan" recipes such as Sautéed Seitan with Green Peas and Mushrooms; Stir-Fried Tofu and Vegetable Teriyaki; and Rapini with Orzo and Sun-Dried Tomatoes. Once your ingredients are assembled, many of these dishes are ready for the table in less than 15 minutes.

In addition to sautés and stir-fries, quick skillet cooking can be utilized to create a number of grain-centered pilafs such as Jasmine Rice Fantasy; Barley Pilaf with White Beans and Broccoli; and Curried Couscous and Vegetables. The speediest pilafs employ quick-cooking grains or grains that have been cooked ahead of time.

sicilian couscous

serves 4

Couscous and raisins are common ingredients in Sicilian cooking. They combine well here with spinach, pine nuts, and a touch of orange, another popular Sicilian ingredient.

2 tablespoons extra-virgin olive oil
2 scallions, minced
3 cups firmly packed fresh baby spinach, chopped
¼ teaspoon red pepper flakes
2 cups vegetable broth (page 15)
1½ cups quick-cooking couscous

¼ cup golden raisins
1 teaspoon grated orange zest
Salt
2 tablespoons chopped fresh parsley
2 tablespoons toasted pine nuts (page 21)

Heat the oil in a large skillet over medium heat. Add the scallions and spinach and cook to soften the scallions and wilt the spinach, 2 to 3 minutes. Stir in the red pepper flakes, then add the broth and bring to a boil. Stir in the couscous and remove from the heat. Stir in the raisins and orange zest, and season to taste with salt. Cover, and let stand for 5 minutes. To serve, sprinkle with the parsley and pine nuts and toss gently to combine.

rapini with orzo and sun-dried tomatoes

serves 4

This recipe is pretty and delicious as is, but it's also extremely versatile. For example, you can substitute spinach or chard for the rapini, and chopped fresh tomatoes for the sun-dried tomatoes. It can also be made with penne or rotini pasta instead of the orzo.

1 bunch rapini (broccoli rabe), coarsely chopped
1½ cups orzo
2 tablespoons extra-virgin olive oil
2 cloves garlic, minced

¼ teaspoon red pepper flakes
⅓ cup chopped oil-packed sun-dried tomatoes
Salt and freshly ground black pepper
¼ cup toasted pine nuts (page 21)

Cook the rapini in a pot of salted boiling water until softened, about 3 minutes. Use a pair of tongs or a slotted spoon to remove the rapini from the water, and set aside.

Return the same pot of water to a boil; add the orzo, stirring occasionally, until it is al dente, about 8 minutes. Drain and set aside.

Heat the oil in a large skillet over medium heat. Add the garlic and cook until fragrant, about 30 seconds. Add the red pepper flakes, sun-dried tomatoes, and reserved rapini. Cook until the rapini is tender, about 5 minutes. Stir in the orzo and season with salt and pepper. Serve sprinkled with the pine nuts.

quinoa pilaf with spinach, apples, and walnuts

serves 4

Walnuts amplify the nutty flavor of the quinoa, while bits of diced apple provide a touch of sweetness.

1½ cups quinoa
3 cups vegetable broth (page 15)
Salt
2 tablespoons extra-virgin olive oil
3 scallions, minced

½ cup walnut pieces
1 (10-ounce) package fresh baby spinach
Freshly ground black pepper
1 apple, halved, cored, and diced

Rinse the quinoa well to remove the bitter white coating. Drain and set aside. Bring the broth to a boil in a saucepan. Decrease the heat to low, add salt if needed, and stir in the quinoa. Cover and simmer until all the water has been absorbed, about 15 minutes.

While the quinoa is cooking, heat the oil in a large skillet over medium heat. Add the scallions and walnuts and cook until fragrant, about 2 minutes. Add the spinach and season to taste with salt and pepper. Cover and cook until wilted, 3 to 5 minutes, then add the apple and cook for 5 minutes more. Stir in the cooked quinoa and taste and adjust the seasonings.

note: You can wilt the spinach in a covered bowl in the microwave, if your skillet is not large enough.

jasmine rice fantasy

serves 4

My wish list of ingredients for a fantasy rice dish includes the evocatively scented jasmine rice combined with flavorful ingredients such as Thai basil, hot chiles, coconut, and cashews. Feel free to make ingredient adjustments to suit your own fantasy. Diced baked tofu is a good addition.

2 tablespoons canola oil
4 scallions, minced
1 cup grated carrot
1 teaspoon fresh or bottled minced ginger
¼ to ½ teaspoon red pepper flakes
2 cups water
2 tablespoons tamari, plus additional to taste

1½ cups jasmine rice
1 cup frozen baby peas, thawed
¼ cup firmly packed fresh Thai basil leaves (see Note)
2 tablespoons roasted cashews
2 tablespoons shredded dried coconut, toasted

Heat the oil in a large skillet over medium heat. Add the scallions and carrot and cook until softened, about 2 minutes. Add the ginger and red pepper flakes, then stir in the water and tamari and bring to a boil. Add the rice, decrease the heat to low, and simmer until tender, about 15 minutes. A few minutes before the rice is cooked, add the peas and basil. Taste and adjust the seasonings, adding more red pepper flakes or tamari, if desired. Serve sprinkled with the cashews and coconut.

note: Thai basil is available in Asian markets. If unavailable, you can either omit it altogether or use another fragrant herb instead, such as regular basil, cilantro, or mint.

quicker fix

This recipe can also be made with cold cooked rice if you have some on hand. You will need about 3 cups of cooked rice; just add the cold cooked rice after you add the ginger and red pepper flakes.

quick stove-top cassoulet

serves 4

About the only thing traditional about this cassoulet is the inclusion of white beans. Where a classic cassoulet contains meat and is generally baked in the oven for an hour or two, this tasty vegetarian version can be on the table in 30 minutes. It begs to be served with hot garlic bread and a crisp green salad.

1 tablespoon extra-virgin olive oil
1 (8-ounce) package vegetarian sausage
   links, cut into 1-inch pieces
1 cup chopped onions
1 cup sliced baby carrots
2 cloves garlic, minced
2 (16-ounce) cans cannellini beans or other
   white beans, drained and rinsed

1 (28-ounce) can diced tomatoes, drained
1 cup vegetable broth (page 15)
1 teaspoon dried thyme
Salt and freshly ground black pepper
1 cup dry bread crumbs

Heat the oil in a large skillet or saucepan over medium heat. Add the sausage and cook until browned, about 5 minutes. Remove the sausage with a slotted spoon and set aside. Put the same skillet back on the heat and add the onions, carrots, and garlic. Cover and cook until softened, about 5 minutes.

Stir in the beans, tomatoes, broth, and thyme. Season to taste with salt and pepper. Cover and cook until the vegetables are tender, about 20 minutes. Stir the cooked sausage into the vegetable and bean mixture.

While the cassoulet is cooking, toast the bread crumbs in a small skillet over medium-high heat, stirring to toast evenly. Be careful not to burn. Set aside. When the cassoulet is ready to serve, top it with the reserved crumbs.

mushroom bulgur pilaf

serves 4

To make this dish even heartier, add a can of white beans when you add the tomatoes, for a soul-satisfying meal in less than 30 minutes. If you buy a package of presliced mushrooms, it will keep prep time to a minimum.

1 tablespoon extra-virgin olive oil
1 teaspoon minced garlic
1 (8-ounce) package sliced mushrooms
1 cup bulgur
2 cups hot vegetable broth (page 15)

Salt and freshly ground black pepper
1 (14-ounce) can petite diced tomatoes, drained
1 tablespoon chopped fresh dill or parsley

Heat the oil in a large skillet over medium heat. Add the garlic and mushrooms and cook until softened, 3 to 5 minutes. Stir in the bulgur, then add the vegetable broth and bring to a boil. Decrease the heat to low and season to taste with salt and pepper. Simmer until the bulgur is tender and the liquid is absorbed, 15 to 20 minutes. Stir in the tomatoes and dill and cook for 3 minutes more to heat through and blend the flavors.

variation

Add a can of drained and rinsed Great Northern or other white beans.

curried couscous and vegetables

serves 4

Talk about curry in a hurry—this flavorful meal can be on the table in minutes. For extra color, add some grated carrot or chopped red bell pepper.

1 tablespoon extra-virgin olive oil
4 scallions, chopped
2 small zucchini, halved lengthwise, and thinly sliced crosswise
1½ tablespoons Madras curry powder, plus additional to taste
½ cup frozen baby peas, thawed

1 (16-ounce) can chickpeas, drained and rinsed
2 cups water or vegetable broth (page 15)
1½ cups quick-cooking couscous
Salt and freshly ground black pepper
¼ cup chopped fresh parsley

Heat the oil in a large skillet over medium heat. Add the scallions and cook, stirring, for 1 minute to soften. Add the zucchini, cover, and cook for 2 minutes to soften slightly. Stir in the curry powder. Add the peas, chickpeas, and water and bring to a boil. Stir in the couscous and season to taste with salt and pepper. If you like it spicier, add more curry powder to taste. Remove from the heat, cover, and let stand for 5 minutes. To serve, fluff the couscous with a fork and transfer to a serving bowl. Sprinkle with the parsley.

joggin' john

serves 4

I call this recipe Joggin' John because it's even quicker to prepare than its inspiration, Hoppin' John, the Southern dish that is said to bring good luck in the New Year. Collards or other dark greens are traditionally served on the side.

2 cups water
1 cup quick-cooking brown rice
Salt
1 tablespoon extra-virgin olive oil
1 Vidalia onion, chopped

1 (8-ounce) package vegetarian sausage links, chopped
2 (16-ounce) cans black-eyed peas, rinsed and drained
Freshly ground black pepper
Tabasco, for serving

Bring the water to a boil in a saucepan, add the rice and salt to taste, and cook until tender, about 10 minutes.

While the rice is cooking, heat the oil in a large skillet over medium-high heat. Add the onion, cover, and cook for 5 minutes, or until the onion is soft. Add the sausage and sauté until browned. Stir in the black-eyed peas, and season with salt and pepper to taste. When the rice is cooked, drain it and stir it into the black-eyed pea mixture. Serve with Tabasco at the table.

barley pilaf with white beans and broccoli

serves 4

Barley is a delicious, nutty, and often overlooked grain. Be sure to get quick-cooking pearl barley for this recipe, since regular barley takes much longer to cook.

2 tablespoons extra-virgin olive oil
½ cup chopped onions
1½ cups vegetable broth (page 15) or water
¾ cup quick-cooking pearl barley

Salt
2 cups small broccoli florets
1 (16-ounce) can Great Northern beans or other white beans, drained and rinsed

Heat the oil in a large skillet over medium heat. Add the onions, cover, and cook until softened, about 5 minutes. Add the broth and barley and bring to a boil. Decrease the heat to low and add salt to taste. (You will need more salt if using water instead of broth.) Cover and simmer for 5 minutes. Add the broccoli, cover, and continue cooking until the broccoli is cooked and the barley is tender, about 5 minutes more. Stir in the beans and heat until hot.

variation

Chopped tomato and dill make good additions.

sautéed cabbage and onions with veggie sausage links

serves 4

Preshredded cabbage cuts down on the prep time for this hearty dish that can be enjoyed in a number of ways. Serve with crusty bread and a side of applesauce, or add some cooked pasta to the skillet after the cabbage is cooked for a hearty one-dish meal. There are a number of different flavors of veggie sausage links available, from spicy Italian, to country-style, to bratwurst-style. Choose whichever one suits your taste. Keep the sausage links whole, or cut into bite-sized chunks, as desired.

2 tablespoons extra-virgin olive oil
1 (8-ounce) package vegetarian sausage
　links
½ cup chopped onions

1 (8-ounce) package shredded cabbage
　(for coleslaw)
Salt and freshly ground black pepper

Heat 1 tablespoon of the oil in a large skillet over medium heat. Add the sausage links and cook until browned, about 5 minutes. Remove from the skillet and set aside, leaving them whole or cutting them into bite-sized pieces.

Heat the remaining 1 tablespoon of oil in the same skillet over medium heat. Add the onions and cabbage and season with salt and pepper to taste. Cover and cook, stirring occasionally, until tender, about 10 minutes. Return the sausage to the skillet to reheat with the cabbage.

variation

Add some cooked rotini, farfalle, or other pasta shape near the end of the cooking time, just long enough to heat through.

pretty quick pinto picadillo

serves 4

Don't be put off by the long list of ingredients in this variation of the classic Mexican dish. Just a few require chopping, and some of those can be bought already cut if you prefer. You can also make this recipe with leftover rice if you have it. For a different taste and texture, frozen veggie burger crumbles can be used to replace the pinto beans.

1½ cups quick-cooking brown rice
1 tablespoon extra-virgin olive oil
½ cup chopped onions
½ cup chopped red or yellow bell pepper
2 garlic cloves, chopped
1 (16-ounce) can pinto beans, drained and rinsed
1 (15-ounce) can petite diced tomatoes, drained
1 Granny Smith apple, halved, cored, and chopped

½ cup raisins
¼ cup sliced pimiento-stuffed green olives
2 tablespoons mild or hot canned chopped green chiles
Salt and freshly ground black pepper
2 tablespoons chopped fresh parsley
2 tablespoons toasted slivered almonds (page 21)

Cook the rice according to package directions. While the rice is cooking, heat the oil in a large skillet over medium heat. Add the onions, bell pepper, and garlic, and cook, stirring occasionally, for 5 minutes, or until the vegetables are soft. Stir in the pintos, tomatoes, apple, raisins, olives, chiles, and salt and pepper to taste. Simmer, stirring occasionally, for 15 minutes, adding a little water if the mixture becomes too dry. To serve, combine the pinto mixture with the hot rice and transfer to a large shallow serving bowl. Garnish with the parsley and almonds.

serving suggestion

Serve the picadillo with guacamole, salsa, and a green salad. It also makes an unusual and tasty filling for burritos.

sautéed seitan with green peas and mushrooms

serves 4

For the quickest prep, pick up a package of presliced mushrooms in the produce section, or procure some from the salad bar. Serve this sauté over brown rice or noodles. For a richer sauce, add some mushroom gravy, store-bought or homemade (page 16).

½ cup unbleached all-purpose flour
½ teaspoon paprika
1 pound seitan, cut into ¼-inch-thick strips
Salt and freshly ground black pepper
2 tablespoons extra-virgin olive oil
2 shallots, minced

2 cups sliced mushrooms
¼ cup dry sherry
¼ cup water or vegetable broth (page 15)
½ teaspoon dried thyme
1 cup frozen baby peas, thawed

Combine the flour with the paprika in a plate or shallow bowl. Season the seitan with salt and pepper and dredge it in the flour mixture. Heat 1 tablespoon of the oil in a large skillet over medium-high heat. Add the seitan and sauté, turning once, until browned on both sides, about 5 minutes. Remove the seitan from the skillet and set aside.

Heat the remaining 1 tablespoon oil in the same skillet, add the shallots, and cook for 2 minutes to soften. Stir in the mushrooms, sherry, water, and thyme. Simmer, stirring, to cook the mushrooms and reduce and thicken the liquid slightly, about 3 minutes. Stir in the peas. Return the seitan to the skillet, season to taste with salt and pepper, and sauté until hot, about 3 minutes.

stir-fried tofu and vegetable teriyaki

serves 4

Some supermarkets carry fresh bagged stir-fry vegetables that can cut down on prep time. Another quick but fresh way to go is grabbing some fresh cut veggies at the supermarket salad bar. Frozen stir-fry vegetables are yet another option.

2 tablespoons canola oil
1 pound extra-firm tofu, cut into
   ½-inch-thick slices
3 scallions, minced
2 cups small broccoli florets
1 cup thinly sliced carrots
½ cup fresh or frozen red bell pepper strips

1 garlic clove, minced
¼ cup freshly squeezed orange juice
¼ cup tamari
2 tablespoons toasted sesame oil
1 tablespoon freshly squeezed lemon juice
1 tablespoon light brown sugar
Salt and freshly ground black pepper

Heat 1 tablespoon of the canola oil in a large skillet over medium heat. Add the tofu and cook, turning once, until golden brown, 8 to 10 minutes. Remove the tofu from the skillet and set aside on a plate.

Heat the remaining 1 tablespoon oil in the same skillet over medium-high heat. Add the scallions, broccoli, carrots, and bell pepper strips, and stir-fry until softened, about 5 minutes. Remove from the heat, add the tofu back into the skillet, and set aside while you prepare the sauce.

In a small bowl, combine the garlic, orange juice, tamari, sesame oil, lemon juice, brown sugar, and salt and pepper to taste. Blend well. Reheat the skillet over medium-high heat. Pour the sauce over the tofu and vegetables and cook, stirring gently, until the tofu and vegetables are hot and well coated with the sauce, about 5 minutes.

quicker fix

Use a bottled teriyaki sauce instead of preparing it from scratch.

seitan with braised radicchio and red onions

serves 4

The slightly bitter taste of radicchio plays nicely against the sweet onions and chewy seitan. Serve on a bed of quinoa or brown rice. (Note: Because the saltiness of the tamari and broth will intensify as the liquid reduces, be judicious in your use of salt in this recipe. Taste for seasonings after the liquid reduces before adding salt.)

3 tablespoons extra-virgin olive oil
1 pound seitan, cut into ¼-inch-thick slices
Salt and freshly ground black pepper
½ cup chopped red onions

1 head radicchio, halved lengthwise
    and cut crosswise into thin strips
½ cup water or vegetable broth (page 15)
1 tablespoon tamari
¼ teaspoon dried thyme

Heat 1 tablespoon of the oil in a large skillet over medium heat. Add the seitan and season with salt and pepper, and cook, turning once, until browned on both sides, 3 to 5 minutes. Remove from the skillet and set aside on a plate.

Heat the remaining 2 tablespoons oil in the same skillet over medium heat. Add the onions and radicchio, cover, and cook until softened, about 5 minutes. Stir in the water, tamari, thyme, and pepper to taste. Add the seitan, cover, and cook until the vegetables are tender, about 10 minutes. If any liquid remains when ready to serve, uncover, turn the heat to medium-high, and cook for another minute, or until the liquid is evaporated.

potato and onion pierogi with broccoli and walnuts

serves 4

Pierogi are Eastern European dumplings similar to ravioli, except that the filling is usually made with potatoes instead of cheese. Frozen pierogi can be found in well-stocked supermarkets.

1 (12-ounce) box frozen potato and onion pierogi
3 cups small broccoli florets
3 tablespoons extra-virgin olive oil

½ cup chopped onions
½ cup walnut pieces
¼ teaspoon red pepper flakes
Salt and freshly ground black pepper

Cook the pierogi and the broccoli in a pot of salted boiling water until the broccoli is just tender, about 5 minutes. Drain well.

Heat 2 tablespoons of the oil in a large skillet over medium heat. Add the onions, cover, and cook until softened, about 5 minutes. Remove the lid, and stir in the walnuts and red pepper flakes. Add the pierogi and broccoli and cook to lightly brown the pierogi, about 5 minutes. Season to taste with salt and pepper and drizzle with the remaining 1 tablespoon olive oil.

note: If pierogi are unavailable, this recipe is also delicious made with a small chewy pasta such as cavatelli or orecchiette.

ingredient alert

Check the ingredient list before you buy. Pierogi may contain dairy products.

panko-crusted tofu cutlets
with lemon-caper sauce

serves 4

Panko is the name for Japanese bread crumbs. Look for them in well-stocked supermarkets.

2 tablespoons tahini (sesame paste)
¼ cup water
Salt and freshly ground black pepper
2 cups panko bread crumbs
3 tablespoons extra-virgin olive oil, plus
  additional as needed
1 pound extra-firm tofu, cut into thin slices
2 shallots, minced

2 tablespoons capers, drained and rinsed
½ cup dry white wine
¼ cup vegetable broth (page 15)
2 tablespoons nonhydrogenated margarine
Juice of 1 lemon
2 tablespoons minced fresh parsley, plus
  additional for garnish

Combine the tahini and water in a shallow bowl until blended. Season with salt and pepper and set aside. Place the panko in a shallow bowl and set aside.

Heat 2 tablespoons of the oil in a large skillet over medium-high heat. Season the tofu slices with salt and pepper to taste, then dip them into the tahini mixture and then into the panko crumbs. Fry the tofu in the hot oil, turning once, until lightly browned, working in batches as necessary. Remove the tofu from the skillet and keep warm.

In the same pan, heat the remaining 1 tablespoon oil. Add the shallots and cook until softened, about 2 minutes. Add the capers, white wine, and vegetable broth and reduce by one-quarter. Stir in the margarine, the lemon juice, and the 2 tablespoons parsley. Add salt and pepper to taste. Pour the sauce over the tofu and garnish with parsley.

tempeh with coconut-peanut sauce

serves 4

The sauce is so yummy, you may want to eat it with a spoon, but save some for the tempeh. This is wonderful served over basmati or jasmine rice. The sauce is also good over tofu or vegetable patties or tossed with noodles.

1 (12-ounce) package tempeh, cut into
  ½-inch-thick slices
2 tablespoons canola oil
2 tablespoons tamari
⅓ cup creamy peanut butter
3 scallions, chopped
2 teaspoons fresh or bottled minced ginger
1 teaspoon minced garlic

¾ cup light unsweetened coconut milk
1 tablespoon freshly squeezed lime juice
1 teaspoon light brown sugar
¼ teaspoon cayenne, plus additional
  to taste
¼ cup chopped peanuts
2 tablespoons minced fresh cilantro

Poach the tempeh in a skillet of simmering water for 7 minutes. Drain and blot dry. Heat the oil in the same skillet over medium-high heat. Add the tempeh and cook until browned on all sides, adding 1 tablespoon of the tamari for color and flavor. Set aside.

In a food processor, combine the peanut butter, scallions, ginger, garlic, coconut milk, lime juice, brown sugar, cayenne, and the remaining 1 tablespoon tamari. Process until smooth, adding more cayenne if you prefer spicier food.

Stir the sauce into the skillet with the tempeh and simmer until hot, about 5 minutes. Serve garnished with the peanuts and cilantro.

quicker fix

If you make this sauce by combining bottled peanut sauce with the coconut milk, you can save time and eliminate several ingredients as well as the need for a food processor.

using your noodle (and pasta)

Simple to make, flavorful, and economical, pasta and noodle dishes can be time-saving treasures and ideal "quick fix" meals. There's no denying that opening a jar of good commercial sauce is by far the fastest way to get a pasta dinner on the table. For that reason, it's a good idea to keep a jar or two of your favorite marinara or other pasta sauce on hand. You can always embellish it with your own touch, such as a splash of wine, or some veggie burger crumbles, to make the sauce taste more like homemade. But when you have a few extra minutes and want a quick-from-scratch sauce that is ready when the pasta is, the recipes in this chapter are just what you need.

Although a particular type of pasta is called for in each recipe, think of it as a suggestion and not written in stone—feel free to mix and match pasta shapes with the different sauces according to your personal preference.

In many cases, the key to getting many of these dishes on the table in less than thirty minutes is to put the pasta water on to boil at the outset, since it can take up to ten minutes for water to come to a boil and then another ten minutes to cook many of the pasta varieties. While the water comes to a boil and the pasta is cooking, you can prepare the sauce and get the rest of dinner ready.

Important: Be sure to put a lid on the pot of water—it will come to a boil more quickly. Add about a teaspoon of salt after the water comes to a boil, not before, as the salt makes the water take longer to boil. And be sure to stir the pasta frequently as it cooks, so it doesn't stick together.

radiatore with chickpeas, baby spinach, and sun-dried tomatoes

serves 4

By the time the pasta is done cooking, your sauce will be ready, tasting like it took a lot more effort to prepare than it actually did. The sun-dried tomatoes add depth to the regular tomatoes and provide a lovely contrast to the vivid green spinach. The addition of meaty chickpeas makes this a delicious one-dish meal. If radiatore ("little radiators") pasta is unavailable, use penne, rotini, or other bite-sized pasta.

1 (10-ounce) package fresh baby spinach
2 tablespoons extra-virgin olive oil
3 cloves garlic, finely chopped
1 (15-ounce) can petite diced tomatoes, drained
⅓ cup oil-packed sun-dried tomatoes, chopped

1 (16-ounce) can chickpeas, drained and rinsed
Salt and freshly ground black pepper
1 pound radiatore or other small pasta shapes

Put the pasta water on to boil in a large covered pot. Place the spinach in a bowl, cover, and microwave for 2 minutes to wilt. Set aside.

Heat the oil in a saucepan over medium heat. Add the garlic and cook until fragrant, about 30 seconds. Stir in both kinds of tomatoes, the wilted spinach, and the chickpeas, and season with salt and pepper to taste. Simmer to blend the flavors and heat through, 5 to 7 minutes.

When the pasta water comes to a boil, salt the water, then add the pasta and cook, stirring occasionally, until it is al dente, 8 to 10 minutes. Drain the pasta and place in a large serving bowl. Add the sauce and toss gently to combine. Serve hot.

spicy ziti with olives and capers

serves 4

Descriptive names for pasta dishes abound in Italy, from spicy arrabbiata, meaning angry or enraged, to the evocative puttanesca, or "streetwalker-style," pasta. By extension, I suppose this delicious recipe, which combines flavor elements of both recipes, could be called "angry streetwalker" pasta.

2 tablespoons extra-virgin olive oil
3 cloves garlic, minced
½ teaspoon red pepper flakes, plus
   additional to taste
1 (28-ounce) can petite diced tomatoes,
   drained

¾ cup pitted Kalamata olives, halved
1 tablespoon capers, drained and rinsed
3 tablespoons chopped fresh parsley
Salt and freshly ground black pepper
1 pound ziti or other small tubular pasta

Put the pasta water on to boil in a large covered pot. Heat the oil in a large skillet over medium heat. Add the garlic and red pepper flakes and cook until fragrant, about 30 seconds. Add the tomatoes and simmer for 10 minutes to allow the flavors to blend. Stir in the olives, capers, parsley, and salt and pepper to taste, adding additional red pepper flakes if you want it spicier. Keep warm over low heat while you cook the pasta.

Cook the ziti in the salted boiling water, stirring occasionally, until it is al dente, about 10 minutes. Drain well and transfer to a shallow serving bowl. Add the sauce and toss to combine.

fusilli and summer vegetables with basil-cannellini sauce

serves 4

Fresh basil combines with cannellini beans for a sauce that envelops the medley of colorful vegetables and chewy fusilli pasta in rich, creamy flavor.

2 large cloves garlic
½ teaspoon salt, plus additional as needed
1 cup firmly packed fresh basil leaves
1 (16-ounce) can cannellini beans, drained and rinsed
3 tablespoons extra-virgin olive oil

1 pound fusilli or other curly pasta
3 scallions, chopped
1 red bell pepper, chopped
1 small zucchini, chopped
1 cup cherry tomatoes, halved
Freshly ground black pepper

Put the pasta water on to boil in a large covered pot. In a food processor, process the garlic with the ½ teaspoon salt. Add the basil and process until minced. Add the beans and 2 tablespoons of the oil and process until smooth. Taste and adjust the seasonings. Set aside.

Salt the water when it comes to a boil, add the fusilli, and cook, stirring occasionally, until it is al dente, about 10 minutes.

While the pasta cooks, heat the remaining 1 tablespoon oil in a saucepan over medium heat. Add the scallions, bell pepper, and zucchini. Cover and cook until softened, about 5 minutes. Add the tomatoes and salt and pepper to taste. Stir in the basil-cannellini sauce and keep warm over very low heat.

When the pasta is cooked, drain it well and transfer it to a shallow serving bowl. Add the vegetables and sauce and toss gently to combine.

penne and roasted asparagus with orange gremolata

serves 4

Traditional gremolata is made with garlic, lemon zest, and parsley and used to sprinkle on Italian stews such as osso bucco. In this recipe, orange zest stands in for the lemons, and the gremolata is used to complement the flavor of roasted asparagus.

1 bunch thin asparagus, cut diagonally into
   1½- inch pieces
¼ cup extra-virgin olive oil, plus additional
   for drizzling
Salt and freshly ground black pepper

1 pound penne pasta
3 cloves garlic, finely minced
½ cup chopped fresh parsley
Grated zest of 2 oranges
3 tablespoons minced scallions

Preheat the oven to 425°F. Put the pasta water on to boil in a large covered pot. Arrange the asparagus in a single layer on a lightly oiled baking pan and drizzle with olive oil. Season with salt and pepper. Roast until just tender, about 8 minutes.

While the asparagus is roasting, cook the penne in the salted boiling water, stirring occasionally, until it is al dente, about 10 minutes.

In a small bowl, combine the garlic, parsley, orange zest, and scallions to create the gremolata, and set aside.

When the pasta is cooked, drain it and place in a large bowl. Sprinkle the gremolata and the ¼ cup olive oil onto the asparagus, stirring gently to combine. Add the asparagus and the gremolata-infused oil to the pasta and toss gently to combine. Serve at once.

farfalle with fresh tomato concassée and black olives

serves 4

Ripe plum tomatoes are used to make the concassée, an uncooked sauce with a slightly chunky texture and a fabulous fresh flavor. If you put the pasta water on to boil as you begin chopping the tomatoes, the pasta will be cooked by the time the sauce is ready to serve.

2½ pounds ripe plum tomatoes
½ cup pitted Kalamata olives, halved
½ cup chopped fresh basil or parsley
1 or 2 cloves garlic, crushed or chopped
   (optional)

Salt and freshly ground black pepper
¼ cup extra-virgin olive oil
1 pound farfalle or other small pasta shapes

Put the pasta water on to boil in a large covered pot. Coarsely chop the tomatoes and place in a large bowl. Add the olives, basil, garlic, and salt and pepper to taste. Drizzle the olive oil over the top and mix gently to combine. Cover and set aside at room temperature for 10 minutes to allow the flavors to blend.

When the pasta water comes to a boil, salt it and add the farfalle. Cook, stirring occasionally, until it is al dente, about 10 minutes. Drain the pasta and place in a shallow serving bowl. Add the sauce and toss gently to combine. Serve at once.

capellini with white bean and green olive tapenade

serves 4

Tapenade is a piquant Mediterranean condiment made with olives and capers. In addition to making a lively pasta sauce, versatile tapenade can be used as a spread for bruschetta or served as a dip with vegetables.

1 cup canned white beans, drained and rinsed
½ cup green olive tapenade, bottled or homemade (page 18)
¼ teaspoon red pepper flakes
¼ cup extra-virgin olive oil
Salt and freshly ground black pepper
1 pound capellini
¼ cup chopped fresh parsley

Put the pasta water on to boil in a large covered pot. In a food processor, combine the beans, tapenade, and red pepper flakes. Process until blended, then add the olive oil and process until smooth. Add salt and pepper to taste. Blend in about ⅓ cup of the hot pasta water to make a smooth sauce. Set aside.

When the pasta water comes to a boil, salt the water, add the capellini, and cook, stirring occasionally, until it is al dente, about 4 minutes. Drain the pasta and place in a shallow serving bowl. Add the tapenade sauce and toss to combine. Serve at once sprinkled with the parsley.

tri-color fettuccine
with rainbow chard,
golden raisins, and pine nuts

serves 4

The vivid orange, pink, and green hues of the chard are played out to dramatic effect with the tri-color pasta noodles. The flavor of this dish is just as delicious with regular fettuccine and Swiss chard (or another leafy green) should the more colorful ingredients be unavailable.

1 bunch rainbow chard, finely chopped
1 pound tri-color fettuccine
⅓ cup extra-virgin olive oil
2 cloves garlic, minced

⅓ cup golden raisins
Salt and freshly ground black pepper
½ cup lightly toasted pine nuts
** (page 21)**

Cook the chard in a large pot of salted boiling water until just tender, about 5 minutes. Scoop out the chard with tongs or a slotted spoon, pat dry, and set aside. Cook the fettuccine in the same pot of boiling water, stirring occasionally, until it is al dente, about 10 minutes.

While the pasta is cooking, heat 2 tablespoons of the oil in a large skillet over medium heat. Add the garlic and cook until softened, about 1 minute. Stir in the raisins and the chard and decrease the heat to low.

When the pasta is cooked, drain well and place in a serving bowl. Drizzle with the remaining olive oil, add the chard and raisin mixture, and season with salt and pepper to taste. Toss gently, and serve at once sprinkled with the pine nuts.

spaghetti with red lentil sauce

serves 4

A key to getting this dish on the table in less than 30 minutes is putting the pasta water on to boil as soon as you begin the recipe. That way the pasta and the sauce will be done at the same time. Alternately, you can make the sauce ahead of time and reheat when ready to use.

2 tablespoons extra-virgin olive oil
1 cup chopped onions
2 teaspoons minced garlic
1 cup red lentils, picked over and rinsed
2 cups hot water or vegetable broth
   (page 15)
Salt

1 (28-ounce) can crushed tomatoes
½ teaspoon dried basil
¼ teaspoon dried oregano or marjoram
¼ teaspoon red pepper flakes
Freshly ground black pepper
1 pound spaghetti
2 tablespoons minced fresh parsley

Put the pasta water on to boil in a large covered pot. Heat the oil in a saucepan over medium heat. Add the onions and garlic. Cover and cook until softened, about 5 minutes. Stir in the lentils, the 2 cups water, and salt to taste. Cover and cook until tender, about 15 minutes. Add the tomatoes, basil, oregano, and red pepper flakes, and season to taste with salt and pepper. Simmer, uncovered, over low heat to blend the flavors, 6 to 8 minutes, or until the pasta is done cooking.

When the pasta water comes to a boil, salt it, add the spaghetti, and cook, stirring occasionally, until it is al dente, about 10 minutes. Drain well. Place the cooked pasta in a shallow serving bowl and spoon the sauce on top and sprinkle with the parsley.

linguine with cherry tomatoes and five-herb pesto

serves 4

Five fragrant herbs combine to create a lush, deep-flavored pesto with its own unique flavor. In Italy, a fresh herb sauce is called *borraccina*. I like to make this sauce when my herb garden is in full swing—it gives me the opportunity to "top" all my plants without decimating any one of them.

2 large cloves garlic
2 scallions, chopped
½ teaspoon salt
½ cup firmly packed fresh parsley leaves
½ cup firmly packed fresh basil leaves
½ cup loosely packed fresh mint leaves
¼ cup loosely packed fresh marjoram leaves

¼ cup loosely packed fresh tarragon leaves
⅓ cup pine nuts or almonds
Freshly ground black pepper
½ cup extra-virgin olive oil
1 pound linguine
2 cups cherry tomatoes, halved

Put the pasta water on to boil in a large covered pot. In a food processor, combine the garlic, scallions, and salt, and process until finely minced. Add the parsley, basil, mint, marjoram, tarragon, and pine nuts, and process until ground to a paste. Add black pepper to taste, and with the machine running, slowly add the olive oil until well blended. Set aside.

Cook the linguine in a large pot of salted boiling water, stirring occasionally, until it is al dente, about 10 minutes. Drain the pasta and place in a shallow serving bowl. Add the sauce and the cherry tomatoes and toss gently to combine. Serve at once.

note: If one or more of the herbs are unavailable, you can substitute a similar herb or double up on an herb you do have.

soba noodles with asian greens and slivers of tofu

serves 4

Buckwheat soba is the basis for this soul-satisfying dish rich in calcium and iron. Buying baked marinated tofu saves preparation time, but you can make your own in advance with regular tofu if you prefer.

1 (10-ounce) package soba (buckwheat) noodles
1 bunch Asian greens (such as bok choy), cut crosswise into ¼-inch chiffonade
1 tablespoon toasted sesame oil
1 tablespoon canola oil

2 cloves garlic, finely minced
½ cup shredded carrot
1 (8-ounce) package baked tofu, cut into thin slivers
2 teaspoons tamari, or to taste
Toasted sesame seeds (page 21)

Cook the noodles in a pot of boiling water until tender, about 5 minutes. During the last minute of the cooking time, add the greens to soften slightly. Drain well and toss with the sesame oil. Set aside.

Heat the canola oil in a large skillet or wok over medium heat. Add the garlic and carrot and stir-fry for 30 seconds. Add the tofu and stir-fry for 1 minute. Add the noodles and greens and the tamari and gently stir-fry until hot, 1 to 2 minutes. Serve sprinkled with toasted sesame seeds.

ginger sesame noodles
with broccoli

serves 4

Instead of linguine, this dish can be made with any variety of Asian noodle you prefer. Either way, it is a satisfying dish that is loaded with flavor. Gomasio is a blend of sesame seeds and sea salt available in natural food stores. It makes a delicious topping for stir-fried dishes such as this one.

2 tablespoons tahini (sesame paste)
1 tablespoon light brown sugar
3 tablespoons mirin
¼ teaspoon red pepper flakes
¼ cup tamari
2 tablespoons water
12 ounces linguine
8 ounces broccoli florets, cut into 1-inch
   pieces

2 tablespoons toasted sesame oil
1 tablespoon canola oil
2 cloves garlic, minced
2 tablespoons fresh or bottled
   minced ginger
Toasted sesame seeds (page 21)
   or gomasio

Put the pasta water on to boil in a large covered pot. In a small bowl, combine the tahini, brown sugar, mirin, and red pepper flakes until well blended. Stir in the tamari and water until blended. Set aside.

When the water comes to a boil, salt it and add the linguine. Cook the linguine until it is al dente, about 10 minutes. During the last 5 minutes of the cooking time, add the broccoli florets and cook until just tender. When the noodles and broccoli are cooked, drain and rinse with cold water. Toss with the sesame oil and set aside.

Heat the canola oil in a large skillet or wok over medium heat. Add the garlic and ginger and stir-fry until fragrant, about 30 seconds. Add the noodles and broccoli and the sauce, and toss to combine and heat through. Serve hot, sprinkled with sesame seeds.

variation

. . . .

Substitute asparagus, cut into 2-inch pieces, for the broccoli.

linguine with edamame pesto

serves 4

East meets West when linguine gets tossed with a vibrant pesto made with edamame, cilantro, and lime juice. Fresh or frozen shelled edamame can be found in well-stocked supermarkets.

1½ cups fresh or frozen shelled edamame
1 pound linguine
1 large clove garlic
½ teaspoon salt

1¼ cups firmly packed fresh cilantro leaves
1 tablespoon freshly squeezed lime juice
½ cup extra-virgin olive oil

Put the pasta water on to boil in a large covered pot. Cook the edamame in a small saucepan of salted boiling water until soft, about 10 minutes. Drain and set aside.

When the pasta water comes to a boil, salt it, add the linguine, and cook, stirring occasionally, until it is al dente, about 10 minutes.

While the pasta is cooking, make the pesto: In a food processor, process the garlic and salt until finely minced. Add the cilantro and puree to a paste. Add the cooked edamame and the lime juice and process until blended. With the machine running, add the oil and process until blended. Add up to ½ cup of the hot pasta water to make a smooth sauce. When the pasta is cooked, drain it and toss with the sauce.

udon noodles and baby bok choy with creamy tahini sauce

serves 4

These long, thick, chewy noodles are made from wheat and are popular in Japanese soups. I think they are also terrific with this tahini sauce.

1 (12-ounce) package udon noodles
2 tablespoons toasted sesame oil
½ cup tahini (sesame paste)
3 tablespoons tamari
¼ cup water or vegetable broth (page 15)
1 tablespoon freshly squeezed lemon juice
1 tablespoon canola oil

2 bunches baby bok choy, thinly sliced crosswise
2 scallions, minced
1 teaspoon fresh or bottled minced ginger
2 tablespoons toasted sesame seeds (page 21)

Cook the noodles in boiling water until tender, about 5 minutes. Drain and place in a bowl. Add 1 tablespoon of the sesame oil and toss to coat. Set aside.

In a small bowl, combine the tahini, tamari, water, and lemon juice until well blended.

Heat the canola oil in a skillet or wok over medium-high heat. Add the bok choy, scallions, and ginger and stir-fry until the bok choy is wilted, about 3 minutes. Stir in the tahini sauce and the noodles and cook, stirring, until heated through, 2 to 3 minutes. Drizzle with the remaining 1 tablespoon sesame oil and serve at once sprinkled with the sesame seeds.

spicy coconut rice noodles with tofu and cilantro

serves 4

Rice noodles range in size from thin vermicelli to the broad flat rice stick noodle. I think the wider noodles stand up better to the sauce. If rice noodles are unavailable, use fettuccine noodles instead.

8 ounces flat rice noodles
2 tablespoons canola oil
8 ounces extra-firm tofu, cut into
   ½-inch dice
2 scallions, chopped
1 teaspoon fresh or bottled minced ginger
½ cup light unsweetened coconut milk

2 tablespoons tamari
1 teaspoon light brown sugar
½ teaspoon red pepper flakes
Salt and freshly ground black pepper
½ cup fresh bean sprouts
¼ cup chopped fresh cilantro

Cook the noodles according to package directions. Drain the noodles and set them aside.

Heat the oil in a skillet or wok over medium-high heat. Add the tofu, scallions, and ginger, and stir-fry until the tofu is golden brown, about 2 minutes. Decrease the heat to low and stir in the coconut milk, tamari, brown sugar, and red pepper flakes. Season with salt and pepper to taste. Add the bean sprouts and cook for 1 minute more. Add the noodles to the skillet and toss gently to combine until heated through. Serve sprinkled with the cilantro.

indonesian-style noodles

serves 4

This popular Indonesian dish is also known as bahmi goreng. Use preshredded cabbage (for coleslaw) and bottled minced ginger for the quickest prep. For a heartier dish, add diced tempeh, seitan, or tofu. I prefer to make this dish with linguine noodles, but you can use Asian noodles, if you prefer.

1 pound linguine
3 tablespoons canola oil
1/2 cup chopped scallions
3 cloves garlic
3 cups shredded cabbage (for coleslaw)

2 teaspoons fresh or bottled minced ginger
1/2 teaspoon red pepper flakes
3 tablespoons tamari
1 teaspoon light brown sugar
2 tablespoons chopped fresh cilantro

Put the pasta water on to boil in a large covered pot. Cook the linguine until it is al dente, about 10 minutes. Drain the noodles well and shake them in a colander to remove any remaining water.

Heat the oil in a large skillet or wok over medium-high heat. Add the noodles and stir-fry until slightly crisp. Remove from the pan and set aside.

To the same skillet, add the scallions, garlic, and cabbage and stir-fry until softened. Stir in the ginger and red pepper flakes, then add the tamari and brown sugar. Return the noodles to the pan and stir-fry to combine and heat through. Serve sprinkled with the cilantro.

chapter 8

one-dish wonders— oven-baked meals

Some evenings our lives can be so hectic that even cooking a quick meal seems like too much effort. Don't reach for the takeout menu just yet. The solution may lie in preparing dinner ahead of time with this special "quick fix" category of oven-baked meals.

From casseroles to pizza and lasagna, these recipes can be assembled in advance—when it's convenient for you—and popped in the oven when you need them. That makes them especially handy to have on hand when you're too busy or tired to cook. Just heat and serve.

In some ways, these recipes can be even easier than the quickest stir-fry or sauté, because all the prep can be done ahead of time, and so can the cleanup.

In addition to serving these dishes on busy weeknights, keep them in mind for company meals as well, so you can put the kitchen mess behind you and have a clean kitchen with no last-minute cooking when guests arrive.

pdq potpie

serves 4

A frozen pie shell comes to the rescue when you want the comforting goodness of a homemade potpie without all the work of making the crust. Using frozen vegetables cuts the prep time further as does using canned mushroom gravy. Check the ingredient labels on the piecrust and gravy: Some brands contain animal products.

1 (16-ounce) package frozen mixed vegetables
1 tablespoon extra-virgin olive oil
½ cup chopped onions
8 ounces extra-firm tofu or other soy "meat," diced*

1 tablespoon minced fresh parsley
½ teaspoon dried thyme
1½ cups mushroom gravy, store-bought or homemade (page 16)
1 frozen deep-dish all-vegetable piecrust, partially thawed**

Preheat the oven to 350°F. Cook the vegetables in a pot of salted boiling water until just tender, about 7 minutes. Drain and transfer to a lightly oiled 2-quart casserole dish.

Heat the oil in a skillet over medium heat. Add the onions and cook, covered, until softened, about 5 minutes. Add to the vegetables in the casserole dish.

In the same skillet, cook the tofu over medium-high heat until lightly browned, about 5 minutes. Add to the vegetables in the casserole dish. Add the parsley, thyme, and gravy, stirring gently to combine.

Place the crust over the filled casserole and crimp the edges onto the dish. Cut three slits in the top of the crust for steam to escape. Bake until the crust is browned and the filling is hot and bubbly, about 45 minutes.

quick-from-scratch note: If you prefer to make your own piecrust and gravy, you can do so ahead of time. Both freeze well, so next time you make either, put some extra in the freezer and you'll have homemade components to use in this "quick-fix" recipe. On page 19 is a recipe for pie dough, including information about piecrusts. On page 16 you will find a recipe for homemade vegetarian mushroom gravy as well as information about store-bought vegetarian mushroom gravy.

*If you're cooking for tofuphobes, you might prefer to dice up a meat alternative such as Morningstar Farms meatless "chicken" strips (available in supermarkets) instead of tofu.

**Just thaw the crust long enough to pop it out of its aluminum pie plate—if you thaw it too long, it will stick to the pie plate and be difficult to get out in one piece.

couscous shepherd's pie

serves 4

A topping of quick-cooking couscous instead of potatoes is one reason this shepherd's pie is ready to pop in the oven in minutes. I like to use frozen veggie burger crumbles in this recipe, but chopped tempeh or tofu may be used instead, if you prefer. For best results, you'll need to sauté either of these first before adding to the recipe.

1 (16-ounce) package frozen mixed
  vegetables
2 cups water or vegetable broth (page 15)
1 cup quick-cooking couscous
Salt
1 tablespoon extra-virgin olive oil
½ cup chopped onions

1 (12-ounce) package frozen vegetarian
  burger crumbles
1½ cups mushroom gravy, store-bought or
  homemade (page 16)
½ teaspoon dried thyme
Freshly ground black pepper
1 tablespoon nonhydrogenated margarine

Preheat the oven to 350°F. Cook the vegetables in a pot of salted boiling water until just tender, about 7 minutes. Drain and transfer to a lightly oiled 2-quart casserole dish.

Bring the 2 cups water to a boil in the same pot in which you cooked the vegetables. Add the couscous and salt to taste. Remove from the heat, cover, and let sit for 5 minutes.

Heat the oil in a small skillet over medium heat. Add the onions, cover, and cook until soft, about 5 minutes. Add to the vegetables in the casserole dish. Stir the burger crumbles into the casserole dish, along with the gravy and thyme. Season to taste with salt and pepper, then spread the couscous evenly on top and dot with margarine. Bake until the filling is hot and bubbly and the top is golden, about 25 minutes.

polenta and pinto bean pie

serves 4

When you use prepared polenta and canned beans, this flavorful casserole can be assembled in just a few minutes. By the time you make a salad and set the table, it's nearly ready to come out of the oven.

1 (16-ounce) package precooked polenta
1 (16-ounce) can pinto beans, drained and rinsed
1 (16-ounce) jar tomato salsa or picante sauce (mild, medium, or hot)

1 (4-ounce) can mild green chiles, drained
1 tablespoon chili powder
Salt and freshly ground black pepper
1 cup shredded soy Cheddar cheese
½ cup crushed tortilla chips

Preheat the oven to 350°F. Cut the polenta into ½-inch-thick slices and arrange in the bottom of a lightly oiled 9- or 10-inch square baking dish. Set aside.

In a bowl, combine the pinto beans, salsa, chiles, and chili powder, and stir to combine. Season with salt and pepper and spread over the polenta.

Top with the shredded soy cheese and the tortilla chips. Cover and bake for 30 minutes. Uncover and bake for 10 minutes more to lightly brown the top.

couscous gratin with peas and pimientos

serves 4

This superquick gratin takes little more than 30 minutes from start to finish—including baking. If you bake it right after assembly, the couscous will still be warm and take only about 20 minutes to bake. If you assemble it ahead of time and refrigerate before baking, allow about 30 minutes to heat through.

2 cups water or vegetable broth (page 15)
1 cup quick-cooking couscous
2 or 3 scallions, minced
1½ cups frozen baby peas
1 (2-ounce) jar chopped pimientos, drained
1 tablespoon extra-virgin olive oil

Salt and freshly ground black pepper
2 tablespoons dry bread crumbs
2 tablespoons grated soy Parmesan (optional)
2 teaspoons nonhydrogenated margarine

Preheat the oven to 350°F. Bring the 2 cups water to a boil. Stir in the couscous, cover, and remove from the heat. Stir in the scallions, peas, pimientos, and olive oil. Season to taste with salt and pepper and let stand for 5 minutes.

Lightly oil a 2-quart gratin dish. Spread the couscous mixture evenly in the dish. Sprinkle the top with the bread crumbs and Parmesan. Dot with the margarine, cover, and bake for 15 minutes. Uncover and continue baking for 5 minutes more, or until the top is lightly browned.

variations

Instead of the peas, substitute 1½ cups of a cooked vegetable such as chopped broccoli, green beans, or asparagus.

beat-the-clock spinach lasagna

serves 4

Soaking the noodles in hot water for a few minutes while you make the filling softens them a bit, then the noodles soften further when they absorb the moisture content in the sauce and filling while the lasagna cooks. Be sure to cover the casserole tightly while it bakes, so no steam escapes. I like the flavor and texture of regular lasagna noodles better than the "no-boil" lasagna noodles, and with this little trick, there's no boiling needed and the lasagna can be assembled in record time.

8 lasagna noodles
1 (10-ounce) package frozen chopped
    spinach, thawed
1 pound firm tofu, drained and crumbled
1 tablespoon freshly squeezed lemon juice
1 teaspoon dried basil

½ teaspoon dried oregano
1 teaspoon salt
¼ teaspoon freshly ground black pepper
1 (24-ounce) jar marinara sauce
½ cup shredded soy mozzarella or grated
    soy Parmesan

Preheat the oven to 350°F. Place the noodles in a long plastic container or a tall heatproof pitcher. (If your container isn't large enough to hold the noodles, you can break them in half to make them fit.) Add just enough hot water to cover the noodles, and set aside.

Squeeze the water out of the spinach and place in a large bowl. Add the tofu, lemon juice, basil, oregano, salt, and pepper. Mix well. Drain the noodles. Do not blot dry.

Spoon a layer of the marinara sauce into the bottom of a 9 by 9-inch baking dish. Top with half of the noodles. Spread half of the tofu mixture evenly over the noodles. Repeat with a layer of the remaining noodles. Top with a thin layer of the sauce and then the remaining tofu mixture, ending with the remaining sauce. Top with the soy cheese. Cover tightly with aluminum foil and bake for 45 minutes. Remove the foil and bake for 10 minutes more. Let stand for 10 minutes before serving.

roasted winter vegetables with seitan chunks and brown gravy

serves 4

This makes good Sunday dinner fare when you don't have time to prepare a special meal. If you have homemade gravy already prepared, this can be assembled in minutes; otherwise, use a commercial mushroom gravy that contains no animal ingredients.

1 cup chopped onions
1 pound baby carrots
2 cups fresh or frozen baby brussels
    sprouts, thawed if frozen, halved if large
1½ pounds fingerling potatoes or small new
    potatoes, halved

2 tablespoons extra-virgin olive oil
1 teaspoon dried thyme
Salt and freshly ground black pepper
8 to 12 ounces seitan, cut into chunks
1½ cups mushroom gravy, store-bought or
    homemade (page 16)

Preheat the oven to 400°F. Lightly oil a large baking dish and spread the onions on the bottom of the dish. Top with the baby carrots, brussels sprouts, and potatoes. Drizzle with the olive oil and sprinkle with the thyme. Season to taste with salt and pepper. Cover tightly and bake until the vegetables are tender, about 1 hour. About 15 minutes before the end of the cooking time, remove the cover and gently stir the vegetables. Add the seitan and gravy. Cover and return to the oven to finish cooking.

note: Additional vegetables and/or seitan may be added as desired.

reinventing the quiche

serves 4 to 6

If ever a recipe was in need of an extreme makeover, it's the quiche. Exit all those high-fat, high-cholesterol ingredients and enter a fabulous new recipe that tastes great, is actually healthy for you, and, best of all, is quick to put together when you use a frozen pie shell.

1 tablespoon extra-virgin olive oil
½ cup minced onions
1½ cups cooked vegetable of choice (see Note)
½ teaspoon salt, plus additional to taste
1 pound extra-firm tofu, drained and crumbled

½ cup soy milk
2 teaspoons Dijon mustard
⅛ teaspoon cayenne
1 frozen deep-dish all-vegetable piecrust, partially thawed, or homemade (page 19)
½ cup shredded soy mozzarella

Preheat the oven to 375°F. Heat the oil in a skillet over medium heat. Add the onions, cover, and cook until softened, about 5 minutes. Add the vegetable of choice and cook if necessary. Otherwise, season with salt to taste, and set aside.

In a food processor, combine the tofu, soy milk, mustard, cayenne, and the ½ teaspoon salt until smooth. Set aside.

If desired, pop the crust out of its aluminum foil pan and place in a fluted quiche pan or pie plate. When thawed enough to manipulate, press the crust into the pan to fit and crimp the edges. Otherwise, keep the crust in its aluminum pan and proceed with the recipe.

Fold the tofu mixture into the vegetable mixture. Stir in the cheese and spread the filling mixture evenly into the bottom of the crust. Bake until firm and lightly browned, about 45 minutes. Allow to cool slightly before cutting.

note: One of the best things about making a quiche is deciding what to put in it. It can be leftover roasted asparagus from last night's dinner, some sliced zucchini or baby spinach that you can sauté with the onion, or maybe some broccoli or frozen artichoke hearts that you can cook in the microwave while you get the rest of the ingredients together. You can even eliminate the veggies and fry up chopped tempeh bacon with onion for a cholesterol-free quiche lorraine.

layered tortilla casserole with guacamole

serves 6

This family-friendly casserole with flavorful layers of refried beans, salsa, and soft tortillas can be quickly assembled ahead of time. If refried beans are unavailable, you can mash a can of drained and rinsed pinto beans.

1 (24-ounce) jar tomato salsa
8 flour tortillas
2 (16-ounce) cans refried beans
1 cup shredded soy Monterey Jack cheese

1 ripe Hass avocado
1 tablespoon freshly squeezed lime juice
Salt and freshly ground black pepper

Preheat the oven to 350°F. Spread a thin layer of salsa in a lightly oiled shallow baking dish. Arrange 4 of the tortillas on top, overlapping as needed.

In a bowl, combine the refried beans with 1 cup of the salsa, stirring to blend well. Spread the bean and salsa mixture over the tortillas and top with ½ cup of the shredded cheese. Arrange the remaining 4 tortillas over the cheese and top with a layer of salsa. Sprinkle the remaining ½ cup cheese on top. Cover and bake until hot, about 30 minutes.

While the casserole is baking, halve and pit the avocado and spoon the flesh into a bowl. Mash the avocado with the lime juice and salt and pepper to taste. Serve with the casserole.

variations

Frozen veggie burger crumbles or soy sour cream may be added to the layers of the casserole.

faster-than-takeout
grilled vegetable pizza

serves 4

It is conceivable that you could actually finish eating your homemade pizza in the time it would take one to be delivered. Best of all, you can control the quality of the ingredients you use, from buying whole grain pizza crusts to using your own inspired toppings.

1 small Japanese eggplant, thinly sliced
2 portobello mushroom caps, thinly sliced
1 small yellow onion, thinly sliced
2 tablespoons extra-virgin olive oil
Salt and freshly ground black pepper
½ teaspoon dried marjoram
½ teaspoon dried basil

1 prebaked 12-inch pizza crust
¾ cup sun-dried tomato hummus (see Variation)
1 ripe tomato, thinly sliced
Optional additional toppings: sliced black olives, sliced cooked or canned artichoke hearts, chopped sun-dried tomatoes

Preheat the oven to 450°F. Preheat the grill or broiler. Toss the eggplant, mushrooms, and onion with the olive oil to coat. Season with salt and pepper. Grill or broil the vegetables until just tender, 5 to 7 minutes. Sprinkle with the marjoram and basil and set aside.

Place the pizza crust on a pizza stone or a lightly oiled pizza pan or baking sheet. Spread the hummus onto the crust, leaving a ½-inch border along the edge. Spread the tomato slices and the grilled vegetables evenly over the hummus. Top with additional toppings if desired. Bake until the pizza is hot and golden brown and the toppings are hot, about 10 minutes.

variation

For a more traditional pizza with tomato sauce, you can omit the hummus and spread the crust with a prepared pizza sauce, available in supermarkets, followed by your favorite toppings.

portobello mushrooms stuffed with artichoke hearts and pine nuts

serves 4

Large, meaty portobello mushrooms make an elegant entrée when stuffed with this flavorful artichoke and pine nut stuffing. Be careful removing the stems so the caps don't break. I like to scrape the bitter-tasting brown gills from the underside of the caps—the mushrooms taste better and it makes more room for the delicious stuffing.

4 large portobello mushrooms, stems chopped and reserved
2 tablespoons extra-virgin olive oil, plus additional needed
Salt and freshly ground black pepper

1 teaspoon minced garlic
1 (6-ounce) jar marinated artichoke hearts, drained, rinsed, and chopped
1 cup dry bread crumbs
¼ cup chopped pine nuts

Preheat the oven to 375°F. Use the tip of a teaspoon to scrape out the brown gills from the underside of the mushroom caps and discard.

Heat 1 tablespoon of the oil in a large skillet over medium-high heat and add the mushroom caps, cut side up, and sear until browned, about 1 minute. Turn over, season with salt and pepper, and cook for 1 minute more. Remove from the skillet and set aside.

Heat the remaining 1 tablespoon oil in the same skillet. Add the garlic and the reserved chopped mushroom stems and cook until softened, about 2 minutes. Stir in the artichoke hearts, bread crumbs, and pine nuts. Remove from the heat. If the filling needs a little moistening to hold together, stir in an additional 1 tablespoon of olive oil or water.

Spoon ½ cup of the stuffing mixture into each mushroom cap and smooth the top. Place the stuffed mushrooms in a lightly oiled baking dish. Bake until hot, about 15 minutes.

zucchini and pesto strata

serves 4

Zucchini, tomatoes, and basil have a natural affinity for one another, as you'll discover when you taste this flavorful strata. The term "strata" refers to a baked dish of layered ingredients that usually includes a layer of bread.

½ cup basil pesto, store-bought or homemade (page 17)
1 cup canned white beans, drained and rinsed
3 tablespoons extra-virgin olive oil
½ cup vegetable broth (page 15)
4 cups cubed day-old French or Italian bread, crusts removed

1½ pounds zucchini, trimmed and thinly sliced
Salt and freshly ground black pepper
4 ripe plum tomatoes, thinly sliced
1 roasted red bell pepper, bottled or homemade (page 20), chopped

Preheat the oven to 375°F. In a food processor, combine the pesto, beans, and 2 tablespoons of the olive oil, and blend until smooth. Add the broth and process until well blended. Set aside.

Spread about two-thirds of the bread cubes in the bottom of a lightly oiled gratin or baking dish and layer half of the zucchini slices on top. Season with salt and pepper to taste. Spoon about half of the pesto sauce onto the zucchini and top with half of the tomato slices. Sprinkle the chopped roasted red pepper over the tomato slices and season with salt and pepper. Top with a layer of the remaining zucchini slices. Season with salt and pepper and top with the remaining pesto, followed by the remaining tomato slices. Season with salt and pepper to taste. Top with the remaining bread and drizzle with the remaining 1 tablespoon olive oil. Cover tightly and bake until the vegetables are tender and bubbly, about 30 minutes.

Remove the lid and bake until the top is lightly browned, about 10 minutes.

baked red beans and rice

serves 4

Using a prepared tomato salsa, with its flavorful bits of onion, bell pepper, and seasonings, helps cut down on the prep time for this easy and satisfying casserole.

1 cup long-grain rice
1¼ cups vegetable broth (page 15)
2 cups tomato salsa
1 (16-ounce) can dark red kidney beans,
   drained and rinsed

½ teaspoon chili powder
Salt and freshly ground black pepper

Preheat the oven to 350°F. Combine the rice and broth in a lightly oiled 2-quart casserole dish. Stir in the salsa, kidney beans, chili powder, and salt and pepper to taste. Cover tightly and bake until the rice is tender, about 1 hour.

quicker fix

· ·

Cut the cooking time in half by heating the vegetable broth and using quick-cooking rice.

serving suggestion

· ·

Serve this casserole with guacamole and a green salad.

chapter 9

slow-cooker
salvation

Like the oven-baked recipes in the preceding chapter, here's another twist on the "quick-fix" idea—slow-cooker recipes. These easy-to-prepare meals literally cook themselves—all it takes is a few minutes of prep time and then you can turn on your slow cooker and let it do all the work. A few hours later, you're rewarded with a home-cooked meal. What could be easier? Many of these recipes also lend themselves to assembling the night before and refrigerating in the slow cooker insert. Come morning, just put the insert in the cooker, turn it on, and when you come home later, dinner is served.

You'll notice that most of these recipes require a few minutes of stove-top cooking in the preparation. Please don't skip this step, because it contributes greatly to the flavor of the finished dish. It's also interesting to note that many vegetarian recipes prepared in a slow-cooker take less time than those made with meat. If you'll be gone longer than the allotted time, consider getting an appliance timer to allow you to adjust your cooking time. For example, you can set it to begin cooking an hour after you leave the house. If you have a "keep warm" setting on your cooker, your meal will be ready and waiting even if you're a little late coming home. For food safety, be sure your food doesn't sit at room temperature longer than two hours.

It's also important to mention that not all cookers heat to the same temperature—some cook faster than others—so please use the ranges of cooking times provided in these recipes as estimates and check the timing using your own cooker the first time you prepare a recipe. You may need to make some adjustments.

one hot potato soup

serves 4 to 6

The beauty of this soup lies in its versatility. As is, it's plain and simple comfort food. Add some fresh herbs, such as rosemary, thyme, or basil, and you can change the character entirely. Leave it chunky for a chowder-style soup, adding some corn kernels, cooked broccoli, or other vegetable. You can also puree the soup for a smooth bisque. If you use leeks instead of garlic, you'll have one hot vichyssoise. Whether left smooth or chunky, you can enliven the flavor at the end with a swirl of pureed chipotle chiles, pesto, harissa, or peanut butter blended with some hot broth.

2 tablespoons extra-virgin olive oil
1 cup chopped celery
2 or 3 cloves garlic, minced
2 pounds Yukon Gold potatoes, diced

4 cups vegetable broth (page 15)
2 cups water
Salt and freshly ground black pepper

Heat the oil in a skillet over medium heat. Add the celery and garlic, cover, and cook until the celery is softened, about 5 minutes.

Transfer the vegetables to a 4-quart slow-cooker. Add the potatoes, broth, water, and salt and pepper to taste. Cover and cook on low until the potatoes are soft, 6 to 8 hours.

When the potatoes are soft, use a potato masher to break up some of the potatoes if desired, or leave as is. Alternately, for a pureed soup, use an immersion blender to puree the soup right in the slow-cooker, or puree the soup in batches in a blender or food processor, returning it to the cooker to keep warm. Taste and adjust the seasonings before serving.

note: Be sure to check this soup for enough salt. The saltiness of your broth and the intensity of any additions to the soup will impact the amount of salt needed.

better than mom's lentil soup

serves 4 to 6

The long, slow cooking brings out the flavors of the ingredients to produce a lentil soup that I once thought to be impossible—one that tastes better than my mom's.

1 tablespoon extra-virgin olive oil
1 cup chopped onions
1 cup sliced baby carrots
½ cup thinly sliced celery
1¼ cups brown lentils, picked over and
   rinsed

1 (15-ounce) can petite diced tomatoes,
   drained
5 cups vegetable broth (page 15) or water
1 tablespoon tamari
Salt and freshly ground black pepper
1 tablespoon minced fresh parsley

Heat the oil in a skillet over medium heat. Add the onions, carrots, and celery. Cover and cook until softened, 7 to 8 minutes. Transfer the vegetables to a 4-quart slow-cooker and add the lentils, tomatoes, broth, and tamari. Cover and cook on low for 6 to 8 hours. Season to taste with salt and pepper. Sprinkle with the parsley when ready to serve.

three-bean soup

serves 4 to 6

It takes a few extra minutes to sauté the onions, garlic, and bell pepper before adding to the slow-cooker, but the payoff is a more flavorful soup. Pureeing a portion of the finished soup also intensifies the flavor as well as giving it a thicker, creamier texture.

1 tablespoon extra-virgin olive oil
½ cup chopped onions
2 cloves garlic, minced
½ cup chopped bell pepper (any color)
½ cup sliced baby carrots
1 (16-ounce) can dark red kidney beans, drained and rinsed
1 (16-ounce) can black beans, drained and rinsed
1 (16-ounce) can cannellini beans or other white beans, drained and rinsed

1 (15-ounce) can diced tomatoes, undrained
4 cups vegetable broth (page 15)
1 bay leaf
½ teaspoon dried thyme
Salt and freshly ground black pepper
¼ cup dry sherry (optional)
2 tablespoons minced fresh parsley or cilantro
Tabasco (optional)

Heat the oil in a skillet over medium heat. Add the onions, garlic, and bell pepper. Cover and cook for 5 minutes to soften. Transfer the onion mixture to a 4-quart slow-cooker. Add the carrots, all of the beans, the tomatoes, broth, bay leaf, thyme, and salt and pepper to taste.

Cover and cook on low for 8 hours. Remove and discard the bay leaf and taste and adjust the seasonings. Add the sherry. Before serving, puree the soup with an immersion blender used right in the cooker, or ladle at least 2 cups of the soup solids into a regular blender or food processor, then puree and stir back into the soup. Serve hot sprinkled with the parsley and a splash of Tabasco, if desired.

brandy-laced french onion soup

serves 4 to 6

The slow-cooker is a natural for making onion soup because it allows the onions to simmer slowly without burning, for a rich and flavorful soup that begs to be served with thick slices of crusty bread.

3 tablespoons extra-virgin olive oil
1 clove garlic, minced
4 cups thinly sliced yellow onions (3 to 4 onions)
¼ cup brandy
3 cups vegetable broth (page 15)

2 cups water
Salt and freshly ground black pepper
1 tablespoon minced fresh parsley
Grated soy Parmesan, for garnish
1 cup croutons, or 4 to 6 slices toasted French bread

Heat the oil in a large saucepan over medium heat. Add the garlic and onions, cover, and cook, stirring occasionally, until softened, about 10 minutes. Stir in the brandy, then transfer to a 4-quart slow-cooker. Add the broth and water. Season to taste with salt and pepper. Cover and cook on high until the onions are very soft, 6 to 8 hours.

To serve, ladle into bowls and sprinkle with the parsley and a dusting of soy Parmesan. Top with the croutons or a slice of toasted French bread.

sweet and spicy stuffed peppers

serves 4

Couscous and chickpeas make an easy and satisfying filling for the peppers, which cook to a delectable softness bathed in a flavorful spicy-sweet tomato sauce. The size of your slow-cooker and the size of the peppers will determine how many stuffed peppers you will be able to fit in your cooker. The stuffing amount provided is enough to fill 4 large peppers.

2 cups water or vegetable broth (page 15)
1 cup quick-cooking couscous
1 (16-ounce) can chickpeas, drained and rinsed
3 scallions, chopped
Salt and freshly ground black pepper

4 large red bell peppers
1 (28-ounce) can crushed tomatoes
2 tablespoons cider vinegar
3 teaspoons light brown sugar
¼ to ½ teaspoon cayenne

Bring the 2 cups water to a boil in a saucepan. Stir in the couscous, chickpeas, scallions, and salt and pepper to taste. Cover and set aside for 5 minutes.

Cut the tops off the bell peppers and remove and discard the stems, seeds, and membranes. Arrange the peppers upright in a slow-cooker. Fill the pepper cavities evenly with the couscous mixture, packing lightly. Replace the pepper tops.

In a medium bowl, combine the tomatoes with the vinegar, brown sugar, cayenne, and salt to taste. Pour the tomato mixture over and around the peppers in the slow-cooker. Cover and cook on low until the peppers are tender but still hold their shape, 4 to 5 hours.

quicker fix

Save a bowl by stirring the vinegar, sugar, cayenne, and salt directly into the open can of tomatoes. If you use a chopstick to mix them in, the tomatoes won't run over the side of the can and there will be no messy bowl to wash.

balsamic-braised seitan and winter vegetables

serves 4

Balsamic vinegar adds a sophisticated depth of flavor to this simple "meat and potatoes" meal. Since food doesn't brown well in a slow-cooker, the ingredients are quickly browned on the stove top before adding to the slow-cooker.

3 tablespoons extra-virgin olive oil
2 small yellow onions, quartered
1 pound baby carrots
1 pound small new potatoes, halved
Salt and freshly ground black pepper

1 (8-ounce) package seitan
2 cloves garlic, crushed
1 teaspoon dried thyme
1 cup water or vegetable broth (page 15)
3 tablespoons balsamic vinegar

Heat 2 tablespoons of the oil in a large skillet over medium-high heat. Add the onions, carrots, and potatoes and brown them quickly. Season the vegetables to taste with salt and pepper and transfer them to a 4-quart slow-cooker.

Heat the remaining 1 tablespoon oil in the same skillet over medium-high heat. Add the seitan and cook until browned, 7 to 10 minutes. Add the garlic and thyme, then stir in the water and vinegar. Use a slotted spoon to add the seitan to the slow-cooker. Reduce the liquid in the skillet by one-third before pouring onto the seitan and vegetables. Cover and cook on low for 6 to 8 hours, until the vegetables are tender. Serve the seitan surrounded by the vegetables and sauce.

five-minute slow-cooker chili

serves 4 to 6

Using chunky salsa eliminates the need for vegetable chopping and helps keep the prep time to a minimum. You can literally put this chili together while walking out the door and come back a few hours later to a luscious meal. Garnish with cooked corn kernels or diced avocado.

1 (24-ounce) jar chunky tomato salsa
2 tablespoons chili powder, plus additional
   to taste
½ cup tomato ketchup
2 (16-ounce) cans black beans, drained and
   rinsed

1 (16-ounce) can dark red kidney beans,
   drained and rinsed
1½ cups water
1 teaspoon salt
¼ teaspoon freshly ground black pepper

Pour the salsa into a 4-quart slow-cooker. Stir in the 2 tablespoons chili powder and the ketchup. Add the black beans, kidney beans, water, salt, and pepper. If you like a spicier chili, add more chili powder. Cover and slow-cook on low for 4 to 6 hours.

variation

Add a 12-ounce package of frozen veggie burger crumbles when you add the beans.

farmers' market stew

serves 4

For a thicker stew, puree up to 2 cups of the solids at the end of the cooking time. For a heartier stew, add a can of chickpeas or other beans or, when ready to serve, sauté a package of sliced veggie sausage links or other veggie "meat."

2 tablespoons extra-virgin olive oil
½ cup chopped onions
1 cup sliced baby carrots
3 cloves garlic, minced
1 pound small red or white potatoes, halved or quartered
1 yellow or red bell pepper, cut into 1-inch pieces
2 zucchini, halved lengthwise and cut into ½-inch slices

1 (15-ounce) can diced tomatoes, drained
2 teaspoons Dijon mustard
1 teaspoon minced fresh or bottled ginger
½ teaspoon paprika
½ teaspoon dried marjoram
2 cups vegetable broth (page 15)
Salt and freshly ground black pepper

Heat the oil in a medium skillet over medium heat. Add the onions, carrots, and garlic. Cover and cook until softened, about 5 minutes. Transfer the vegetables to a 4-quart slow-cooker. Add the potatoes, bell pepper, zucchini, and tomatoes. In a small bowl, combine the mustard, ginger, paprika, and marjoram. Stir in a small amount of vegetable broth to blend and then add to the cooker along with the remaining broth and salt and pepper to taste. Cover and cook on low for 6 to 8 hours, until the vegetables are tender.

jamaican red bean stew

serves 4 to 6

This hearty stew will fill your home with the fragrant scent of island cooking. This recipe doesn't require any separate pans, since the small amount of garlic has time to mellow in the oil right in the cooker while you prepare the remaining ingredients.

1 tablespoon extra-virgin olive oil
2 cloves garlic, minced
2 cups sliced baby carrots
3 scallions, chopped
1 sweet potato, diced
1 (15-ounce) can diced tomatoes, drained
2 teaspoons curry powder
½ teaspoon dried thyme

¼ teaspoon red pepper flakes
¼ teaspoon ground allspice
Salt and freshly ground black pepper
2 (16-ounce) cans dark red kidney beans, drained and rinsed
1 (14-ounce) can unsweetened light coconut milk
1 cup vegetable broth (page 15)

Pour the oil into a 4-quart slow-cooker and set the cooker on high. Add the garlic and put the lid on the cooker while you prepare the rest of the ingredients.

To the cooker, add the carrots, scallions, sweet potato, and tomatoes. Stir in the curry powder, thyme, red pepper flakes, allspice, and salt and pepper to taste. Add the beans, coconut milk, and broth. Reduce heat, cover, and cook on low for 6 to 8 hours.

serving suggestion
. . . .
Serve over rice or couscous.

slow-cooked layered vegetables

serves 4

For a gratin-like topping, just before serving, top with toasted bread crumbs and grated soy cheese. Herbes de Provence, a fragrant blending of herbs common to the south of France, usually contains basil, marjoram, fennel seeds, thyme, savory, rosemary, and sometimes lavender.

3 tablespoons extra-virgin olive oil
1 cup chopped onions
1 (15-ounce) can petite diced tomatoes, drained
1 cup chopped red bell pepper
1 teaspoon dried herbes de Provence or other dried herbs of choice

Salt and freshly ground black pepper
1 Yukon Gold potato or russet potato, cut into ¼-inch slices
3 cups firmly packed fresh baby spinach
1 sweet potato, cut into ¼-inch slices
½ cup vegetable broth (page 15)

Heat 2 tablespoons of the oil in a large skillet over medium heat. Add the onions, cover, and cook until softened, about 5 minutes. Transfer the onions to the bottom of a 4-quart slow-cooker. Top with half the tomatoes and then half the bell pepper, and season with a pinch of the herbs, and salt and pepper to taste. Layer half the potato slices on top, followed by half the spinach, then half the sweet potato, seasoning each layer with salt and pepper to taste. Top with layers of the remaining tomatoes, bell pepper, potato, spinach, and sweet potato. Pour in the vegetable broth and drizzle on the remaining 1 tablespoon olive oil. Cover and cook on low for 6 to 8 hours, until the vegetables are tender.

indian-style vegetable stew

serves 4

I like to serve this fragrant stew over freshly cooked basmati rice.

2 tablespoons extra-virgin olive oil
1 cup chopped onions
1 cup chopped carrots
½ cup chopped celery
2 cloves garlic, minced
1 tablespoon fresh or bottled minced ginger
1 bunch scallions, chopped
½ teaspoon ground cumin
½ teaspoon ground cinnamon

½ teaspoon ground cardamom
2 potatoes, diced
1 (16-ounce) can chickpeas, drained and
    rinsed
2 cups water or vegetable broth (page 15)
Salt and freshly ground black pepper
1 (10-ounce) package fresh baby spinach
Chopped cilantro and chopped tomato,
    for garnish

Heat the oil in a skillet over medium heat. Add the onions, carrots, and celery. Stir in the garlic, ginger, scallions, cumin, cinnamon, and cardamom. Cover and cook until the vegetables are softened, about 5 minutes. Transfer to a 4-quart slow-cooker. Add the potatoes, chickpeas, water, and salt and pepper to taste. Cover and cook on low for 6 to 8 hours, until the vegetables are tender. About 15 minutes before ready to serve, stir in the spinach. When ready to serve, garnish with chopped cilantro and tomato.

garden vegetable strata

serves 4

Layers of flavorful vegetables are slowly cooked in a creamy tomato sauce. The best part of making this strata in a slow-cooker is that it doesn't heat up the kitchen when you make it during hot weather and, of course, it allows you to go out and play in the sun (or work) while it cooks.

1 clove garlic
½ teaspoon salt, plus additional as needed
1 cup canned white beans, drained and rinsed
1 (15-ounce) can diced tomatoes, drained
½ cup water
2 tablespoons extra-virgin olive oil
½ teaspoon dried basil
1 cup chopped onions

½ cup chopped red or yellow bell pepper
1 fennel bulb, chopped
½ loaf French or Italian bread, crust removed
1½ pounds zucchini, thinly sliced
Freshly ground black pepper
1 russet potato, thinly sliced
Toasted bread crumbs, for garnish

In a blender or food processor, combine the garlic and the ½ teaspoon salt and process until the garlic is minced. Add the beans, tomatoes, water, 1 tablespoon of the olive oil, and the basil. Blend until smooth and set aside.

In a large skillet, heat the remaining 1 tablespoon oil over medium heat. Add the onions, bell pepper, and fennel. Cover and cook until softened, 5 to 7 minutes. Remove the skillet from the heat and set aside.

Slice the bread and arrange it in the bottom of a lightly oiled 4- to 5-quart slow-cooker and layer half of the zucchini slices on top. Season with salt and pepper to taste. Spoon about one-quarter of the tomato–white bean sauce onto the zucchini and top with half of the potato slices. Season with salt and pepper to taste and top with a layer of half of the onion-fennel mixture spread evenly. Top with a layer of the remaining zucchini slices. Season with salt and pepper and top with one-quarter of the tomato-bean sauce. Top with the remaining potato slices and season with salt and pepper to taste, followed by one-quarter more of the sauce, the remaining onion-fennel mixture, and then the remaining sauce. Season with salt and pepper to taste. Put the lid on the slow-cooker and cook on low until the vegetables are tender, 6 to 8 hours. When ready to serve, garnish with toasted bread crumbs.

quick brown rice–stuffed buttercup squash

serves 4

The size and shape of your slow-cooker will dictate whether you cook this squash whole or in 2 halves. If you have a large oval cooker, you can cut the squash in half and set the halves side by side, stuffed side up, in the cooker. If you have a smaller round cooker, be sure to find a squash that will fit inside it whole.

1½ cups quick-cooking brown rice
1 large buttercup squash
1 tablespoon extra-virgin olive oil
4 scallions, minced
½ cup chopped walnut pieces

1 teaspoon dried thyme or sage
½ cup sweetened dried cranberries
1 tablespoon minced fresh parsley
Salt and freshly ground black pepper
1 cup water, hot

Cook the rice according to package directions—it should take about 10 minutes. While the rice is cooking, prepare the squash (see Note). If using whole, slice off a few inches from the top and scoop out the seeds. If halving, cut in half and remove the seeds. Set aside.

Heat the oil in a large skillet over medium heat. Add the scallions and walnuts and stir until fragrant, about 3 minutes. Stir in the thyme, then add the cranberries, parsley, and the cooked rice. Season with salt and pepper to taste. Mix well and spoon the mixture into the squash.

Pour the hot water into a slow-cooker, and add the squash, stuffed side up. Cover and cook on low until the squash is tender, 6 to 8 hours.

note: To make cutting into a hard squash easier, put it in the microwave for a few minutes to soften the skin slightly.

chunky fresh pear and apple sauce with cranberries

makes about 4 cups

This is worth making just for the fragrance that fills your house while it is cooking, but you'll also be rewarded with a delicious fresh-tasting side dish that will make you wonder why you ever ate canned applesauce. (Note: If you prefer a basic [but delicious] applesauce, simply omit the cranberries and pears and double up on the apples.)

4 cooking apples, halved, cored, and diced
4 ripe pears, halved, cored, and diced
½ cup light brown sugar
½ cup water

1 tablespoon freshly squeezed lemon juice
1 teaspoon ground cinnamon
½ teaspoon ground ginger
⅓ cup sweetened dried cranberries

Combine the apples, pears, brown sugar, water, lemon juice, cinnamon, and ginger in a 4-quart slow-cooker. Cover and cook on low for 4 to 6 hours, until the fruit is very soft. Mash gently with a potato masher to break up slightly. Stir in the cranberries. Serve warm or allow to cool.

serving suggestions

You can serve this as a side dish in the same way you would serve applesauce or cranberry sauce. It is especially good as an accompaniment to the Roasted Winter Vegetables with Seitan Chunks and Brown Gravy on page 142 or the Seitan with Braised Radicchio and Red Onions on page 110.

chapter 10

sauces in a snap

Sometimes just the right sauce can be the secret to a sensational meal. And it doesn't have to take a lot of effort, even if you make a sauce from scratch. Among the advantages of a homemade sauce over a store-bought one is that it can be more economical to make, you can season it to your taste, and you can avoid the stabilizers and other additives found in many commercial products.

The recipes in this chapter are ideal for cooks who prefer homemade sauces but don't have all day to make them. From a rich red wine sauce to a garlicky white bean skordalia, these versatile sauces can literally make the meal. Still, there are times when you need a sauce in seconds, not minutes. For those occasions, there is a wide variety of ready-made sauces at the supermarket. You can find bottled, canned, and packaged sauces ranging from tomato sauces and pestos, to salsas and tapenades, to peanut sauces, chutneys, gravies, and much more.

When buying commercial sauces, it's important to find brands you like, since the flavor and quality can vary greatly among brands. Sometimes a little doctoring is all that is needed to turn a so-so sauce into one that is sensational.

Note: In addition to the sauce recipes in this chapter you can find recipes for Basic Basil Pesto, Mushroom Gravy, and Tapenade in chapter 1 beginning on page 16. Those recipes are located in the "basics" chapter because they are called for frequently in other recipes throughout this book.

fast tomato salsa—your way

makes about 2 cups

With commercial salsas available in an amazing number of flavors and types, the quickest fix is to buy a jar of salsa at the store. Still, many of us prefer to "have it our way" but want a quick, easy scratch salsa that doesn't take a lot of time. The ideal salsa is one that is made with fresh ripe tomatoes and other just-picked veggies from the garden. The sad reality is many of us don't have access to fresh tomatoes most of the year and the ones that are available often taste like cardboard. To address this issue, a combination of canned and fresh tomatoes are used in this recipe. Feel free to adjust as necessary either way depending on the availability of fresh tomatoes.

2 ripe tomatoes, chopped
¼ cup chopped red onion
1 (15-ounce) can petite diced tomatoes, drained
1 (4-ounce) can chopped mild green chiles
1 chopped chipotle chile in adobo sauce, canned (optional)

1 tablespoon extra-virgin olive oil
2 tablespoons freshly squeezed lemon juice or cider vinegar
½ teaspoon sugar
½ teaspoon salt

Combine all the ingredients in a bowl. Mix well, cover, and refrigerate for at least 1 hour or overnight to blend the flavors. For a smoother salsa, combine the ingredients in a food processor and pulse until the sauce reaches the desired consistency.

variations

Opportunities abound for personal touches. Omit the chipotle chile, or use hot green chiles instead of mild chiles, gauging the amount according to your own preference. You can use all fresh tomatoes or all canned tomatoes, or add some minced garlic, cilantro, or parsley. Add black beans and corn kernels for another tasty variation.

serving suggestions

In addition to serving this salsa as a dip for tortilla chips, you can use it to make the Guacamole Roll-Ups on page 25, the Creamy Tortilla Soup on page 43, or the Polenta and Pinto Pie on page 139.

roasted red pepper sauce

makes about 1½ cups

When you use bottled roasted red peppers, this sauce takes just minutes to make. Vibrant in both color and flavor, it is terrific served with roasted vegetables or added to sauce or pasta dishes. Served cold, it can also be used to dress salads.

1 tablespoon extra-virgin olive oil
1 clove garlic, chopped
1 (6-ounce) jar roasted red bell peppers,
   drained and coarsely chopped
½ cup diced tomato

1 tablespoon red wine vinegar
½ teaspoon sugar
¼ teaspoon salt
⅛ teaspoon cayenne
¼ cup water

Heat the oil in a small saucepan over medium heat. Add the garlic and cook until fragrant, about 30 seconds. Stir in the roasted red peppers and tomato and cook, stirring occasionally, for 5 minutes. Add the vinegar, sugar, salt, and cayenne and simmer for 5 minutes more to blend the flavors.

Transfer the mixture to a food processor and puree until smooth, adding the water as necessary for the desired consistency. Taste and adjust the seasonings. Serve hot or cold.

serving suggestions

Try it as a dressing for the Black Bean and Rice Salad with Roasted Red Peppers and Corn on page 63 or in place of the tomato concassée in the Farfalle with Fresh Tomato Concassée and Black Olives on page 122.

spinach-walnut pesto

makes about 1½ cups

This pesto is a nice change from basil pesto and especially practical to make when fresh basil is not plentiful. Made with iron- and calcium-rich spinach and walnuts, this pesto is also a nutritional dynamo. Walnut oil is especially good in this, if you have some on hand.

3 cups fresh spinach
3 cloves garlic
1 teaspoon salt

1 cup firmly packed fresh parsley leaves
⅓ cup walnut pieces
⅓ cup extra-virgin olive oil or walnut oil

Steam the spinach over boiling water for 1 minute, or wilt it in a covered bowl in the microwave for about 3 minutes. Mince the garlic with the salt in a food processor. Squeeze any moisture from the spinach and add to the food processor along with the parsley and walnuts. Puree until smooth. Add the olive oil gradually and process to a smooth paste.

serving suggestion

Toss with cooked pasta, adding a little of the hot pasta water to thin the sauce.

meyer lemon sauce

makes about 1 cup

This is a versatile and flavorful sauce that can be used in a number of ways. Try it as a salad dressing or dip. Warm it and serve as a sauce for tofu, tempeh, or steamed or roasted vegetables. It can also be used on cooked grain and noodle dishes. The sauce is easily doubled and can be made thinner or thicker, depending on how much water you add. If Meyer lemons are unavailable, another lemon variety may be used.

¼ **cup tahini (sesame paste)**
1 teaspoon minced garlic
¼ **cup freshly squeezed Meyer lemon juice**
2 tablespoons tamari
1 tablespoon water, plus additional as needed

2 tablespoons toasted sesame oil
Salt and freshly ground black pepper
2 tablespoons minced fresh parsley

In a large bowl, combine the tahini, garlic, lemon juice, tamari, and water. Whisk together to blend. Whisk in the sesame oil. Blend well. Taste and adjust the seasonings, and season with salt and pepper to taste. Stir in the parsley, adding more water if needed to achieve the desired consistency.

serving suggestion

Toss this sauce with soba (buckwheat) noodles, minced scallions, and toasted sesame seeds. Add some steamed broccoli or asparagus for a light yet satisfying meal.

harissa in a hurry

makes about 1 cup

This fiery sauce can be made quickly when you use bottled roasted red bell peppers and ground spices. If you prefer to begin with whole spices, you can toast the whole spices in the same manner as directed below, and grind them in a spice grinder before adding to the recipe. Choose the number of dried hot chiles to use according to your own heat tolerance.

One advantage of making your own harissa sauce is that you can control the amount of heat. Another advantage is that this spicy North African condiment can be difficult to find other than in specialty markets and gourmet grocers. It can be used to flavor soups or stews such as vegetable tagines. It's also a zesty condiment for tofu or veggie burgers or an addition to soy mayonnaise if you want to add some extra heat and flavor. A little goes a long way.

2 dried hot red chiles, stemmed and seeded
1 teaspoon ground caraway
1½ teaspoons ground coriander
½ teaspoon ground cumin
3 cloves garlic
½ teaspoon salt

1 roasted red bell pepper, bottled or homemade (page 20)
1 tablespoon extra-virgin olive oil
3 tablespoons water
1 teaspoon white wine vinegar

Break the dried chiles into pieces. Place in a heatproof bowl and cover with boiling water. Soak for 10 minutes while you gather the remaining ingredients. Drain. Do not pat dry.

Toast the caraway, coriander, and cumin in a small skillet over low heat until fragrant, 1 to 2 minutes, stirring frequently so the mixture doesn't burn. Remove from the heat.

In a food processor, mince the garlic with the salt and toasted spices. Add the roasted red pepper, the soaked dried chiles, and the olive oil, and puree until smooth. Add the water and vinegar and puree to a smooth paste. The sauce is now ready to use or can be stored in the refrigerator in a container with a tight-fitting lid until needed. Properly stored, the harissa will keep for several weeks.

rich red wine sauce

makes about 1 cup

This sauce may take a few minutes longer to make than the others, but the results are worth the effort. If the sauce looks more red than brown, you can deepen the color with a small amount of gravy browning liquid, available in supermarkets.

1 tablespoon extra-virgin olive oil
¼ cup chopped onion
¼ cup chopped carrot
1 teaspoon chopped garlic
½ cup chopped mushrooms
1 cup dry red wine
1 cup vegetable broth (page 15) or water
1 tablespoon tamari

¼ teaspoon crumbled dried thyme
Salt and freshly ground black pepper
1 tablespoon cornstarch dissolved in 2
   tablespoons water
½ teaspoon gravy browning liquid, such
   as GravyMaster or Kitchen Bouquet
   (optional)

Heat the olive oil in a saucepan over medium heat. Add the onion, carrot, garlic, and mushrooms. Cover and cook to soften slightly, about 3 minutes. Stir in the wine, broth, tamari, and thyme. Simmer, uncovered, until the liquid is reduced by nearly half, about 10 minutes.

Strain the reduced sauce into a saucepan, pressing on the solids with the back of a spoon. Season to taste with salt and pepper. Return the saucepan to the burner and simmer over medium heat. Whisk in the cornstarch mixture, stirring to thicken slightly, about 5 minutes. If a darker brown color is desired, stir in up to ½ teaspoon of browning liquid. Serve hot.

serving suggestion

I like to add this sauce to sautéed seitan and mushrooms and serve over rice or noodles.

creamy mustard dipping sauce

makes about ¾ cup

This zesty and flavorful sauce shines as a dipping sauce for steamed or fried vegetables, baked tofu or tempeh nuggets, fried spring rolls, or soft pretzels. It's also great on sandwiches and veggie burgers.

½ cup soy mayonnaise
3 tablespoons Dijon mustard

3 tablespoons yellow mustard
1 teaspoon Tabasco

Combine all the ingredients in a food processor or blender until smooth and well blended.

ginger coconut sauce

makes about 1 cup

Use this exotic fragrant sauce to enliven rice and noodle dishes or as a stir-fry sauce for vegetables, tofu, or tempeh.

2 teaspoons canola oil
2 tablespoons grated fresh ginger
1 teaspoon minced garlic
1 teaspoon light brown sugar
½ teaspoon Asian chili paste

1 cup light unsweetened coconut milk
Salt
1 teaspoon cornstarch dissolved in
   1 tablespoon water

Heat the canola oil in a saucepan over medium heat. Add the ginger, garlic, and brown sugar, and cook, stirring, until fragrant, about 30 seconds. Stir in the chili paste, coconut milk, and salt to taste. Bring just to a boil, then decrease the heat to low, stir in the cornstarch mixture, and cook until thickened, about 3 minutes. Taste and adjust the seasonings.

black bean sauce with sherry

makes about 1½ cups

This quick and easy sauce adds flavor to grain dishes and is great as a topping for vegetable patties or veggie burgers.

1 tablespoon extra-virgin olive oil

2 cloves garlic, chopped

1 (16-ounce) can black beans, drained and rinsed

¼ teaspoon ground cumin

2 tablespoons tamari

2 tablespoons dry sherry

2 tablespoons water, plus additional as needed

1 tablespoon freshly squeezed lemon or lime juice

Salt and freshly ground pepper

½ teaspoon hot pepper sauce (optional)

2 tablespoons chopped fresh cilantro

Heat the olive oil in a saucepan over medium heat. Add the garlic and cook until fragrant, about 30 seconds. Stir in the beans, cumin, tamari, sherry, and water and simmer for about 5 minutes to blend the flavors. Transfer the mixture to a blender or food processor, add the lemon juice, and blend until smooth. Return to the saucepan and season to taste with salt and pepper and the hot sauce. Stir in the cilantro and add more water if the sauce is too thick. Simmer, stirring, until hot.

golden garbanzo sauce

makes about 2 cups

The rich golden color and light flavor of this sauce makes it especially appealing over cooked vegetables. Try it on mashed potatoes for a real treat.

1 tablespoon extra-virgin olive oil
2 tablespoons chopped yellow onions
2 tablespoons dry white wine
1 (16-ounce) can chickpeas (garbanzo beans), drained and rinsed
½ cup vegetable broth (page 15)

2 tablespoons tahini (sesame paste)
1 tablespoon white miso paste
1 tablespoon freshly squeezed lemon juice
Salt
Cayenne

Heat the olive oil in a saucepan over medium heat. Add the onions, cover, and cook until softened, about 3 minutes. Stir in the wine, beans, and vegetable broth and simmer for 2 minutes to blend the flavors. Transfer the mixture to a blender or food processor. Add the tahini, miso, lemon juice, and salt and cayenne to taste. Blend until smooth and creamy. Return the sauce to the saucepan and heat over low heat until hot, stirring frequently.

creamy chutney-cashew sauce

makes about 1 cup

This spicy-sweet sauce can transform an ordinary pasta or rice salad into one that is truly sensational. It also makes a yummy topping for baked tofu or tempeh.

¼ cup cashew nuts
½ cup water
½ cup mango chutney

Grind the cashews to a powder in a dry blender. Add the water and process until smooth. Add the chutney and puree until smooth.

white bean and almond skordalia

makes about 2 cups

The classic Greek garlic sauce is often made with potatoes or bread, sometimes with the addition of almonds or walnuts. My version combines white beans and almonds for a protein-rich and superquick sauce.

1 cup chopped almonds
6 cloves garlic, minced
1 (16-ounce) can Great Northern beans or
   other white beans, drained and rinsed

Juice of 1 lemon
¼ cup white wine vinegar
1 cup extra-virgin olive oil
Salt and freshly ground black pepper

In a dry blender or food processor, grind the nuts to a powder. Add the garlic and process until smooth. Add the beans and process until smooth and well combined. Add the lemon juice and vinegar. With the machine running, slowly add the olive oil until the mixture is smooth. The sauce should be creamy and thick. Season to taste with salt and pepper. If the sauce is too thick, add a little cold water (up to ¼ cup).

serving suggestions

Use as a sauce for grilled vegetables, tofu, or seitan. Swirl some into soups for added flavor, or use it as a dip for raw vegetables or pita bread. You might also try it on a sandwich or in a wrap as a flavorful alternative to mayonnaise.

no-fuss
desserts

Everyone loves a good homemade dessert, and while most of us don't have the time or inclination to bake our own elaborate cakes and tortes, there are less complicated ways to get a delicious homemade dessert on the table.

Between the extremes of a made-from-scratch pastry creation and a package of convenience-store cupcakes lies a group of no-fuss desserts that require a minimum of ingredients, preparation, and cooking. These shortcut desserts employ a maximum of improvisation, flair, and presentation, as well as helpful ingredients such as ready-made puff pastry and piecrusts and easy dessert sauces.

In addition to preparing these simple and speedy recipes, don't forget to keep your favorite frozen desserts on hand to scoop into pretty dessert dishes. Add a delicious sauce, some chopped toasted nuts, or some fresh fruit and a mint sprig, and you can serve your own signature dessert in minutes.

no-bake oatmeal cookies with almonds and dried cranberries

makes about 2 dozen

When there's no time to bake, these tasty cookies can be assembled quickly and then popped in the refrigerator to firm up. Loaded with flavor, the hardest part is not eating them all in one sitting.

¾ cup almond butter
½ cup confectioners' sugar
3 tablespoons cranberry juice or water
1 teaspoon pure vanilla extract
1½ cups rolled oats (quick-cooking
   or old-fashioned)

½ cup sweetened dried cranberries
¼ cup sliced or slivered almonds, toasted
   (page 21)

In a large bowl, combine the almond butter, sugar, juice, and vanilla. Mix well. Stir in the oatmeal, cranberries, and almonds. Mix until well combined.

Drop by rounded teaspoonfuls onto cookie sheets lined with wax paper. Use your hand or the tines of a fork to flatten. Set aside or refrigerate for 1 hour to allow the cookies to firm up a bit.

variations

The almond butter can be replaced with peanut butter or another nut butter of your choice. Instead of dried cranberries, try dried cherries or golden raisins. Add some chocolate chips if desired.

pecan shortbread cookies

makes about 20

With just four ingredients and only minutes to bake, even the busiest person can put these fresh-baked cookies on the table.

¾ cup pecan pieces, toasted (page 21)
½ cup nonhydrogenated margarine, chilled

½ cup sugar
1 cup unbleached all-purpose flour

Preheat the oven to 350°F. Grind the pecans in a food processor. Add the margarine and sugar and process until well combined. Add the flour and pulse to combine.

Shape the dough into 1-inch balls and arrange on a nonstick cookie sheet, about ½ inch apart. Press the dough balls with the tines of a fork to flatten. Bake until golden brown, 12 to 15 minutes. Allow to cool before eating.

favorite fruit crisp

serves 4 to 6

This crisp is called "favorite" because that's what you use—your favorite fruit, which to me is whatever is in season at the moment. This crisp cooks up especially fast with a softer fruit such as peaches, so that's what is used here, but harder fruits such as apples may be used, although they'll need to bake a bit longer, even if they are sliced extremely thin. For the quickest fruit crisp of all, use canned fruit or fruit pie filling. Serve warm with a scoop of your favorite frozen dessert or a drizzle of Secret Vanilla Sauce (page 201).

6 ripe peaches (or your favorite fruit)
½ cup light brown sugar
1 teaspoon ground cinnamon
1 tablespoon cornstarch

⅓ cup old-fashioned rolled oats
⅓ cup unbleached all-purpose flour
⅓ cup nonhydrogenated margarine

Preheat the oven to 400°F. Lightly oil an 8-inch square baking dish or coat with nonstick cooking spray. Thinly slice the peaches and place them in the prepared baking dish. Mix in ¼ cup of the brown sugar, ½ teaspoon of the cinnamon, and the cornstarch.

In a bowl, combine the oats, the flour, the remaining ¼ cup brown sugar, the remaining ½ teaspoon cinnamon, and the margarine. Mix with a pastry blender until the texture resembles coarse crumbs.
Sprinkle the topping over the fruit in the baking dish. Bake until the topping is golden brown and the fruit bubbles in the center, about 20 minutes. To serve, spoon the crisp into dessert dishes while still warm.

quicker fix

Use frozen or canned fruit or a can of fruit pie filling instead of fresh fruit. If using pie filling, omit the cornstarch and the ¼ cup of brown sugar for the filling.

tropical mango pastry purses

serves 4

These little pastry bundles taste like fresh mango pie and are as cute as can be. Quick and easy, too, thanks to frozen puff pastry. Allowing two per person, serve them nestled next to a scoop of your favorite frozen dessert, or dress them up with a drizzle of melted chocolate or fresh berry coulis.

1 sheet frozen puff pastry, thawed
2 large ripe mangoes, halved and pitted
2 tablespoons sweetened shredded dried
  coconut

2 tablespoons crushed peanuts
¼ teaspoon sugar
Confectioners' sugar or Fresh Berry Coulis
  (page 200), for garnish

Preheat the oven to 400°F. Roll out the puff pastry sheet on a lightly floured work surface, to about a 9-inch square. Cut the pastry into 4 pieces, each about 4½ inches square.

Chop the mangoes and divide among the pastry, placing a spoonful in the center of each pastry square. Top the mangoes with a sprinkling of coconut and nuts and a pinch of sugar. Gather the corners of the pastry squares together and pinch them together to envelop the filling. Twist the corners of each pastry together so it looks like a little bundle. Repeat until all the bundles are sealed.

Place the pastry purses on a nonstick baking sheet and bake until golden brown, 12 to 15 minutes. Serve warm with a dusting of confectioners' sugar or on a pool of berry coulis.

rustic plum tart

serves 6

This free-form tart, called a galette, is made even easier with the help of a frozen piecrust. If you prefer to make your own piecrust (page 19), proceed with this recipe after you roll out your dough.

1 frozen deep-dish piecrust, thawed
3 cups sliced ripe plums
1 teaspoon nonhydrogenated margarine

1 tablespoon sugar
½ teaspoon ground cinnamon

Preheat the oven to 425°F. Carefully place the crust on a lightly floured surface. Lightly flour a rolling pin and roll the crust out into a flat circle, about 12 inches in diameter. Transfer the crust to a baking sheet and arrange the sliced plums in a circle on the crust, leaving a 2-inch edge. Fold the exposed edge of the crust up around the plums, pinching the edges of the dough together. The plums in the center of the tart will remain visible.

Dot the plums with the margarine. Combine the sugar and cinnamon and sprinkle on top. Bake until the fruit is bubbly and the crust is golden brown, 20 to 25 minutes. Remove from the oven and allow to cool slightly. This tastes best when served warm.

variations

Use a different ripe fruit such as peach or pear. Adjust the baking time as necessary.

quicker fix

Use canned or frozen fruit or a canned fruit pie filling instead of fresh fruit.

chocolate–peanut butter pastry packets

serves 4 to 8

Keep puff pastry in the freezer for impromptu company desserts. These pastry packets taste like chocolate croissants and look lovely on a pool of berry coulis, nestled with a scoop of vanilla ice cream. For added texture, use chunky peanut butter or add some chopped nuts to the filling.

1 sheet frozen puff pastry, thawed
¾ cup creamy peanut butter
¾ cup semisweet chocolate chips

Confectioners' sugar or Fresh Berry Coulis (page 200)

Preheat the oven to 400°F. Roll out the puff pastry sheet on a lightly floured work surface, to measure about 9 by 12 inches. Cut the pastry into 3-inch squares. Place a heaping teaspoonful of peanut butter on each pastry square, followed by a spoonful of the chocolate chips.

Fold each pastry square in half diagonally, moistening the edges with a bit of water and pressing to seal. For a decorative finish, press along the seam edges with the tines of a fork. Repeat until all the packets are sealed.

Place the pastry packets on a nonstick baking sheet and bake until golden brown, 12 to 15 minutes. Serve warm with a dusting of confectioners' sugar or, better yet, on a pool of berry coulis, allowing one or two packets per person depending on appetites.

lemon sorbet pie with toasted almonds and fresh berries

serves 8

This versatile pie is refreshing, sophisticated, and oh so easy. Change the flavor of the sorbet, crust, and fruit according to your preference. Instead of topping with nuts, you can top with fresh fruit of choice, or serve with a fruit sauce. Allow at least 4 to 6 hours in the freezer before serving.

1 ½ cups vanilla cookie crumbs (about 20 small cookies)
3 tablespoons nonhydrogenated margarine, melted

1 quart lemon sorbet, softened
1 cup sliced almonds, toasted (page 21)
2 cups ripe strawberries, raspberries, or blueberries

Lightly coat a 9-inch springform pan with nonstick cooking spray. Place the cookie crumbs and melted margarine in the prepared pan and mix to moisten the crumbs. Press the crumb mixture into the bottom and up the sides of the pan. Set aside.

In a bowl, stir the softened sorbet until smooth. Spoon into prepared crust, spreading with a rubber spatula to flatten the top. Freeze for several hours or overnight.

When ready to serve, carefully remove the sides from the pan and top the pie with the toasted almonds. If serving whole, place on a platter and surround with the fresh berries. If plating individually, cut the pie and place the pieces on dessert plates. Arrange a large spoonful of the fruit decoratively next to each slice of pie.

variation

Use lime sorbet and a gingersnap crust—top with sliced ripe mango and a pool of pureed mango.

quicker fix

Instead of crushing cookies to make the crumb crust, buy a ready-to-use graham cracker or vanilla cookie crumb crust.

ingredient alert

Be sure to check the ingredients of these crusts as they may contain dairy products.

pineapple-apricot couscous cake

serves 6

This couscous cake is one of those easy and versatile recipes that lend themselves to a variety of toppings, from sliced fresh seasonal fruit, to a fruit coulis, to toasted nuts and a drizzle of chocolate.

2 cups pineapple juice
1 cup quick-cooking couscous
2 dried apricots, snipped into tiny pieces
1/3 cup crushed pineapple, drained

1 tablespoon light brown sugar
1/2 teaspoon ground cinnamon
Pineapple-Apricot Sauce (page 203)

Bring the pineapple juice to a boil in a saucepan. Add the couscous, apricots, pineapple, brown sugar, and cinnamon. Decrease the heat to low, cover, and simmer until the juice is absorbed, about 5 minutes.

Press the mixture into a lightly oiled 9-inch springform pan. Cover loosely and refrigerate for at least 1 hour.

To serve, cut into wedges and top each slice with a spoonful of the Pineapple-Apricot Sauce.

quicker fix

Instead of topping with the Pineapple-Apricot Sauce, buy a jar of ice cream topping from the supermarket—pineapple, walnut, or chocolate sauce would be especially good.

banana-pecan fantasy

serves 4

This is my version of bananas Foster, a luscious dessert created at Brennan's Restaurant in New Orleans, where bananas, butter, and brown sugar converge with banana liqueur and rum, which is traditionally flambéed and served over vanilla ice cream. My version pares down the calories and cancels the cholesterol of the original but retains its deliciously decadent flavor. And I also add pecans to my version for extra texture and flavor—hey, it's my fantasy! Be sure your ice cream is prescooped and your dessert dishes are ready to go, because this dessert comes together quickly and should be served while the bananas and sauce are still warm and before the ice cream melts.

4 scoops vanilla or pecan soy ice cream (try Tofutti Better Pecan)
¼ cup nonhydrogenated margarine
½ cup light brown sugar

½ cup pecan pieces
4 ripe bananas, sliced
¼ cup dark rum

Scoop the ice cream into individual serving dishes and place in the freezer. Combine the margarine, sugar, and pecans in a large skillet over medium heat. Cook, stirring, until the sugar dissolves, 2 to 3 minutes. Add the bananas and cook until slightly browned and softened, 1 to 2 minutes. Carefully add the rum. Continue to cook the sauce until the rum is hot, about 1 minute. Spoon the bananas and sauce over the ice cream in the serving dishes. Serve immediately.

blushing poached pears with walnuts and cranberries

serves 4

I usually don't like to "cook" with the microwave, but there are a few things that it does really well in a hurry, and poaching pears is one of them. If you prefer to poach your pears on top of the stove, you can do so, but it will take around 30 minutes for the pears to soften.

½ cup sweetened dried cranberries
½ cup walnut pieces
1½ cups cranberry juice

1 tablespoon dry red wine (optional)
2 Bosc pears, ripe but not too soft

Combine the cranberries, the walnuts, 1 cup of the cranberry juice, and the wine in a saucepan and bring to a boil. Decrease the heat to medium and cook until the liquid becomes syrupy, about 10 minutes.

While the mixture is simmering, prepare the pears. Halve the pears and scoop out the center with a melon baller to remove the center core and create a small hollow. Place the pear halves in a microwave-safe dish and pour the remaining ½ cup cranberry juice over the pears. Cover and microwave on high until softened, about 6 minutes.

Arrange the poached pears on a serving dish and use a slotted spoon to fill with the cranberry-walnut mixture. Drizzle the remaining syrup over all.

chocolate-cherry truffles

makes about 3 dozen

These rich-tasting truffles look adorable when presented in little foil or paper candy cups. Use a high-quality cocoa for best results. Dried cranberries or blueberries may be substituted for the cherries if desired.

¼ cup dried cherries
½ cup almond butter, at room temperature
2 cups confectioners' sugar
½ cup cocoa

1 teaspoon pure vanilla extract
Coating of choice: unsweetened cocoa, crushed toasted almonds, toasted shredded coconut

Place the cherries in a heatproof bowl and cover with ¼ cup boiling water to soften. Drain the cherries and transfer to a food processor and process until finely chopped. Add the almond butter and process until smooth. Add the confectioners' sugar, cocoa, and vanilla. Blend well, then transfer to a bowl.

Using your hands, roll a small amount of the mixture into a 1-inch ball. Repeat until the mixture is used up. Drop the truffles, 2 or 3 at a time, into a shallow plate containing either cocoa, almonds, or coconut, depending on your preference. Roll the truffles in the coating, covering completely and pressing the coating lightly onto the truffles. Transfer to a plate and refrigerate until firm. Store in an airtight container in the refrigerator.

chocolate-banana pudding

serves 4

This creamy and delicious pudding has a nice balance of chocolate and banana flavors and the buttery texture of cashew crème.

1 cup semisweet chocolate chips
½ cup raw cashews
⅓ cup water

2 ripe bananas
¼ cup pure maple syrup
1 teaspoon pure vanilla extract

Melt the chocolate in a double boiler over low heat, stirring constantly. Set aside. In a blender or food processor, grind the cashews to a powder. Add the water and blend until smooth. Add the bananas, maple syrup, and vanilla, and blend until smooth. Add the melted chocolate and process until smooth.

Transfer to individual serving bowls or glasses. Cover and refrigerate until well chilled.

skewered fruit with a trio of dipping sauces

serves 4

Serving these gorgeous skewers of grilled fruit with three different sauces creates maximum visual impact for very little effort. If using bamboo skewers, be sure to soak them in water for 30 minutes to prevent burning.

1 cup ripe strawberries
½ pineapple, cored and cut into 1-inch chunks
3 ripe peaches or apricots, halved, pitted, and cut into chunks

1 cup large seedless grapes (red or white)
3 dessert sauces of choice (see Note)

Preheat the grill. Skewer the fruit onto the skewers in an alternating pattern and grill on both sides, just until grill marks start to appear, about 5 minutes each side.

To serve, arrange the skewered fruit on a large platter with pitchers or bowls of the dessert sauces alongside. To serve plated, place 1 or 2 skewers of fruit on an individual plate with 3 tiny bowls of sauce for each person. (Plates and small bowls used for sushi look lovely for this purpose.)

note: If you want to make your own sauces, good choices include Pineapple-Apricot Sauce (page 203), Dark Chocolate Yum Sauce (page 202), Secret Vanilla Sauce (page 201), and Fresh Berry Coulis (page 200).

quicker fix

Instead of making your own dessert sauces, buy ready-made sauces at the supermarket, such as those to top ice cream sundaes, available in chocolate, pineapple, strawberry, and other flavors.

fresh berry coulis

makes about 1½ cups

If fresh berries are unavailable, use thawed frozen berries. Lemon juice brings out the natural sweetness of the berries.

2 cups ripe raspberries or strawberries
1 to 2 tablespoons superfine sugar
½ teaspoon freshly squeezed lemon juice

Combine the berries, sugar, and lemon juice in a blender or food processor and puree until smooth. Pour the mixture through a fine-mesh strainer into a bowl, pressing on the solids. Cover and refrigerate until needed.

secret vanilla sauce

makes 1 cup

This sauce is too easy and too delicious to keep a secret for long. The first time I made it, it was one of those happy accidents. Now I make it on purpose, embellishing it with fruit purees, extracts, or whatever else will complement the rest of the dessert it's being served with. I use soy ice cream for a guilt-free, cholesterol-free treat.

1 cup vanilla soy ice cream (Tofutti works great for this; see Note)

Place the ice cream in a bowl and set aside at room temperature until melted. Stir until smooth. The sauce is now ready to use.

note: Melt as much ice cream as you will need, depending on the number of people you are serving. Allow about ¼ cup per person.

dark chocolate yum sauce

makes about 1 cup

This sauce is as good as the chocolate used to make it, so go for a quality brand. Coconut milk adds a rich flavor dimension.

½ cup light unsweetened coconut milk
2 tablespoons sugar
2 tablespoons pure maple syrup

6 ounces bittersweet chocolate, chopped
1 teaspoon pure vanilla extract

In a saucepan, bring the coconut milk, sugar, and maple syrup to a simmer. Remove from the heat. Add the chocolate. Whisk until the chocolate is melted and the sauce is smooth. Whisk in the vanilla extract. Serve at once.

pineapple-apricot sauce

makes about 2 cups

This luscious sauce has a glorious golden color and tastes more complex than it is. It's a perfect match for the Pineapple-Apricot Couscous Cake on page 194, but it is also terrific on pound cake or soy ice cream, or as a dipping sauce for fruit.

¾ **cup dried apricots**
¾ **cup water**
½ **cup crushed pineapple**

In small saucepan, combine the apricots and water. Cover and bring to a boil. Remove the lid, lower the heat, and simmer until the apricots are soft and the liquid reduces slightly, about 15 minutes. Remove from the stove and allow the mixture to cool slightly. Transfer the mixture to a blender or food processor and puree until smooth. Add the pineapple and blend again until smooth.

index